THE AUL' DAYS

THE AUL' DAYS

EWAN FORBES

ABERDEEN UNIVERSITY PRESS

First published 1984
Aberdeen University Press
A member of the Pergamon Group

© Sir Ewan Forbes 1984

British Library Cataloguing in Publication Data

Forbes, *Sir* Ewan
  The aul' days.
  1. Forbes, Ewan   2. Scotland — Biography
  I. Title
  941.1082'092'4   CT828.F6

  ISBN 0-08-030409-5
  ISBN 0-08-032415-0 Pbk

F5
FOR
——
3.
507402

Printed in Great Britain
The University Press
Aberdeen

To my wife

CONTENTS

ACKNOWLEDGEMENTS

If it had not been for the pressing encouragement of my old and revered friend, that great Doctor of Literature, A. R. B. Haldane, C.B.E., D.Litt, LL.B., this book would never have been written. He always said 'you have so much knowledge of History and Country lore, you must write'. I always protested that although I was a raconteur, I had no gift for writing. I was always enchanted by his beautiful descriptions about the country in 'The Drove Roads' and the tremendous amount of information about nature and the old customs of our land. Eventually, last winter, the inspiration came over me to try, and I found writing the reminiscences was quite easy. I am much indebted to him for his inspiration. My thanks are due to his widow for her advice about publishing, and in great measure to Mrs. Margaret Rogie for typing my script. I would like to extend my grateful thanks to the North East of Scotland Library Service and to their colleagues in Renfrewshire for supplying me with copies of the Statistical Accounts of Scotland. I am grateful to all the wonderful characters like the Bain family, who have been tenants of the Forbeses of Craigievar for over 500 years, and finally to my wife who has taken such an interest in all the country lore and been my help at all times.

FAMILY OF CORSE AND CRAIGIEVAR

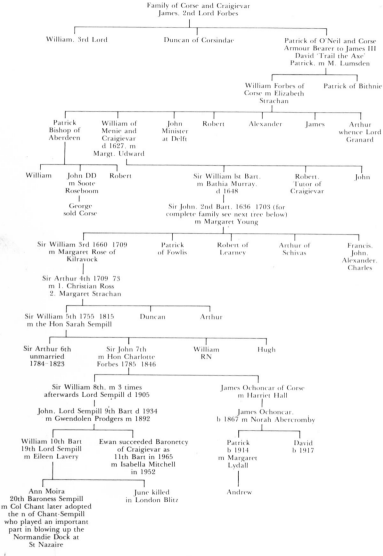

Family of Corse and Craigievar
James. 2nd Lord Forbes

William. 3rd Lord

Duncan of Corsindae

Patrick of O'Neil and Corse
Armour Bearer to James III
David 'Trail the Axe'
Patrick. m M. Lumsden

William Forbes of
Corse m Elizabeth
Strachan

Patrick of Bithnie

Patrick
Bishop of
Aberdeen

William of
Menie and
Craigievar
d 1627. m
Margt. Udward

John
Minister
at Delft

Robert

Alexander

James

Arthur
whence Lord
Granard

William

John DD
m Soote
Roseboom

Robert

Sir William 1st Bart.
m Bathia Murray.
d 1648

Robert.
Tutor of
Craigievar

John

George
sold Corse

Sir John. 2nd Bart. 1636 1703 (for
complete family see next tree below)
m Margaret Young

Sir William 3rd 1660 1709
m Margaret Rose of
Kilravock

Patrick
of Fowlis

Robert of
Learney

Arthur of
Schivas

Francis.
John.
Alexander.
Charles

Sir Arthur 4th 1709 73
m 1. Christian Ross
2. Margaret Strachan

Sir William 5th 1755 1815
m the Hon Sarah Sempill

Duncan

Arthur

Sir Arthur 6th
unmarried
1784 1823

Sir John 7th
m Hon Charlotte
Forbes 1785 1846

William
RN

Hugh

Sir William 8th. m 3 times
afterwards Lord Sempill d 1905

James Ochoncar of Corse
m Harriet Hall

John. Lord Sempill 9th Bart d 1934
m Gwendolen Prodgers m 1892

James Ochoncar.
b 1867 m Norah Abercromby

William 10th Bart
19th Lord Sempill
m Eileen Lavery

Ewan succeeded Baronetcy
of Craigievar as
11th Bart in 1965
m Isabella Mitchell
in 1952

Patrick
b 1914
m Margaret
Lydall

David
b 1917

Ann Moira
20th Baroness Sempill
m Col Chant later adopted
the n of Chant-Sempill
who played an important
part in blowing up the
Normandie Dock at
St Nazaire

June killed
in London Blitz

Andrew

X

MY BEGINNING

In the 1880s my parents met in Homburg where so many people of the merry and fashionable world used to go. Nearly all these spas were popularised by the Prince of Wales, later Edward VII and became holiday resorts with concert halls and casinos. My father was a Scot, in fact the heir to the Highland estate which includes the famous Castle of Craigievar. On the other side of the Highland line was an excellent arable and wooded estate with a large solid granite house built in 1824 by my great-grandfather, who was a second son and succeeded his brother who died without issue. My great-grandfather was a man of great force and purpose and was employed by the Honourable East India Company, as a Judge. On the death of his brother, he returned to Scotland and set to work, first to save Craigievar Castle by re-roofing it. If it had not been for his care and foresight, it might well have been a ruin today. At Fintray, he pulled down the old house which was a long single-storied building and erected what was termed a large and commodious mansion with bathrooms and remarkable plumbing for the age. My mother realised no doubt, that the existence of Fintray House was the reason that no additions were built on to Craigievar which would have spoiled the original design in the interest of accommodating endless staff to suit the living standards of the times. As it is, I believe that it is the oldest inhabited and unaltered castle in Scotland, and a gem of Scottish Baronial architecture.

During the meeting of my parents in Homburg they became engaged and were married on 22 June 1892. My mother was of Welsh extraction of the old family of Ap Roger of Gwarrindee in Monmouthshire. They were descended originally from 'Herbert the Chancellor' who came over with William the Conqueror in 1066 springing from Pepin Count of Vermandois and through Pepin King of Italy from Charlemagne. During the reign of the Stewart dynasty after the union of the Crowns, they held many household positions at Court, but unfortunately the English contracted their name to Prodgers. My

1

Craigievar Castle.

Fintray House.

Terraces of Fintray House.

mother was proud of her Welsh descent and was a character of great fortitude and determination and blessed with a wonderful sense of humour. She was, true to her nation, very musical and artistic. She played five instruments, but her favourite was undoubtedly the harp. She was a pupil of the great Welshman Thomas, and I remember her telling me of a wonderful concert in the Queen's Hall, London with about thirty harpists who were pupils of this famous musician and composer. Many years later, in the 1930s, I was invited to take my team of Scottish Country Dancers to perform in the Queen's Hall, which brought happy reminiscences to my mother of her concert days.

She was adamant that having married a Highland Laird, she must accept his 'plaidie' and give all her loyalty to Scotland and her husband. She learned to speak the Doric and even endeavoured to teach those in ignorance of the language a few practical sentences. I remember one — 'Dinna dicht yer nib wi yon cloutie'!

My bringing up was strict and just, and cures for coughs, colds, flu and other ailments very tough. She had a 6-ounce bottle of clear brown fluid which was produced as a powerful cure for all ills, and with the orders to take a dose forthwith, she announced with great confidence, 'Of course it will cure you, it saved the life of your father's horse in the South African War.' It was known as Globena and tasted pleasant at the first gentle sip, but on taking a mouthful, one choked on the burning ginger. However, it was always successful! For sprains and other injuries, Elliman's Embrocation as prepared for horses was always used.

My father's career was soldiering which started with the Gordon Militia at the old King Street, Barracks in Aberdeen. In the South African War he served with the Lovat Scouts but eventually joined the family regiment, the Black Watch. Early in World War I he received a telegram from Kitchener asking him to command the 8th Battalion Black Watch. He told me he was the first man to land in France from K.I. as he jumped on to the quay just before the gangway was secured. He was severely wounded through the spine at Loos, which ended his war career.

My father's generation suffered severely in India and World War I. His second brother was killed in the North West Frontier of India in 1908 when a Major in the Seaforths. His third brother, apart from one who died in infancy, was a peace-loving and artistic civilian, who worked with the Bombay Burmah trading corporation, but of course joined up with the Gordons at the beginning of the war and was killed on the Somme. The youngest, serving in the Navy, escaped injury at Jutland. In many ways my father was rather disinterested in his family with the exception of being very particular about proper Scottish upbringing as taught by his father, with an insistence on being able to speak, read and write the Doric so that Scottish literature and verse could be fully enjoyed, and having a close understanding with all true residents of the land. He considered that inability to do so displayed apathy and ignorance of our race. Two or three European languages were also expected as, in bygone days, the Scots were largely dependent on trade and friendship with France and the Hanseatic League and were not often at peace with England. It was not to be said that we were less well-educated than our forbears had been. One was always expected to make strangers feel at home.

Willie the Merchant or Danzig Willie who was a younger son of the Laird of Corse ultimately made a substantial fortune in trading and acquired the lands of Menie, Fintray and Craigievar in Aberdeenshire and also lands in Fife. He belonged to a family strong in support of the Reformation (when his eldest son succeeded and was created a Baronet of Nova Scotia on 20 April 1630). He built Craigievar Castle (started by the Mortimers in early 1600), completing it in 1626, and establishing it as a stronghold of the Scottish Presbyterian Faith. When Charles I caused Bishop Laud to try and establish the English Book of Common Prayer upon the Scots — the story of Jenny Geddes in St Giles is well-known there was uproar at this outrage. Hundreds upon hundreds of supporters of the Kirk of Scotland met in Greyfriars Kirk in Edinburgh and signed the Covenant. Sir William Forbes 1st Bart of Craigievar, became a leader of the Covenanters and led the

Ewan Forbes, present Baronet, wearing the Insignia of the Baronetcy of Nova Scotia Forbes of Craigievar. The insignia bear the arms of Nova Scotia surmounted by the Crown with the inscription FAX MENTIS HONESTAE GLORIA hung on an orange ribbon. The Baronetcy of Craigievar is one of the earliest created and was granted by the King with 16,000 acres of land in Nova Scotia.

The Honourable SIR EWAN FORBES OF CRAIGIEVAR, Baronet. Baron of Brux in the County of Aberdeen (formerly the Honourable Sir Ewan Forbes of Brux, Baronet). Holder of the Degrees of Bachelor of Medicine and Bachelor of Surgery of the University of Aberdeen, residing at Brux, Alford in the County of Aberdeen, having by Petition unto the Lord Lyon King of Arms of date 26 March 1977, SHEWN: THAT he, the Petitioner (who is the second son of the late the Right Honourable Sir John Forbes-Sempill, 18th Lord Sempill in the Peerage of Scotland, and a Representative Peer, 9th Baronet Forbes of Craigievar in the ——— Baronetcy of Nova Scotia, and his wife (married 22 June 1892) Gwendoline Emily Mary, elder daughter of Herbert Bridges of ——— Kingston St. Michael in Wiltshire: THAT the Petitioner's said father (born 21 August 1863) was the eldest son of the Right Honourable Sir William Forbes-Sempill (formerly Sir William Forbes) of Craigievar in the County of Aberdeen, 8th Baronet, 17th Lord Sempill in the Peerage of Scotland, who of date 16 July 1885 recorded his armorial bearings in the Public Register of All Arms and Bearings in Scotland (Volume 11, Folio 61) being therein described as elder son of the late Sir John Forbes of Craigievar, Baronet, whose armorial bearings were recorded in the said Public Register (Volume 4, Folio 70) of date 12 March 1843: ——— WHICH said Sir John Forbes of Craigievar was son and eventually heir of Sir William Forbes of Craigievar, Baronet, and his wife Sarah, daughter of John, Lord Sempill: WHICH said John, Lord Sempill, was great-grandson of Robert, Lord Sempill, whose armorial bearings were recorded in the said Public Register circa 1672: THAT the Petitioner's older ——— brother, the Right Honourable William Francis Forbes-Sempill, 19th Lord Sempill, died 30 December 1965 and, having no male issue, was succeeded in the Peerage by his eldest daughter, the Right Honourable Ann Moira Sempill, Baroness Sempill: THAT ——— on the death without male issue of the said 19th Lord Sempill, the Petitioner became entitled to matriculate the arms of Forbes of Craigievar without brisure or mark of cadency: AND the Petitioner having prayed that the foresaid Ensigns Armorial of Forbes of Craigievar might be matriculated of new in his own name without brisure or mark of cadency together with the additaments appropriate to him as a Baronet of Nova Scotia and Baron of Brux: The Lord Lyon King of Arms by Interlocutor of date 29 March 1977, Granted Warrant to the Lyon Clerk to matriculate in the Public Register of All Arms and Bearings in Scotland in name of the Petitioner the following Ensigns Armorial, VIDELICET: ——— Azure, a cross patée fitchée Or between three bear's heads couped Argent, muzzled Gules. Above the shield, behind which is draped his studio-burnial mantle Gules doubled of silk Argent, fur-edged of miniver and collar Ermine and fastened on the right shoulder by five spherical buttons Or, is placed a chapeau Gules furred Ermine (for his feudal barony of Brux) thereon is placed an helmet befitting his degree with a Mantling Azure doubled Or and on a Wreath of the liveries is set for Crest A cock proper, and in an Escrol over the same this Motto "WATCH." Upon a compartment below the shield which is ensued with an orange-tawny ribbon and pendent therefrom the Badge of a Baronet of Nova Scotia, are placed for supporters, on the dexter side a Knight in armour of the fifteenth century, armed at all points, having the beaver of his helmet up and leaning on a shield Or charged with a lion rampant Gules armed and langued Azure within a double tressure flowered and counterflowered with fleurs-de-lis of the second, and on the sinister a Bear Argent, muzzled Gules. ———

Matriculation of the arms of The Honourable Sir Ewan Forbes of Craigievar, Baronet, showing the Nova Scotia Insignia incorporated with the Barony of Brux. It thus pertains specifically to the author alone.

charge against Montrose in Aberdeen. He was twice taken prisoner but was steadfast in his belief and swore on Oath to the Lord, that if any of his sons or those who succeeded to the Baronetcy of Craigievar should forsake the Presbyterian Faith and the covenant, the Lands of Craigievar would surely be taken from them. It therefore came about that each Baronet of succession took this oath until the 10th Baronet who ultimately became a Roman Catholic. The prediction of the Covenanters was fulfilled and the lands were indeed taken away. My brother married Eileen Lavery the daughther of the famous artist Sir John Lavery. She was beautiful, charming, clever and Irish. She was also a Roman Catholic, but never sought to cause anyone to be influenced by her own private beliefs. My father worried about the succession, but as there were only two lovely daughters of the marriage this did not affect the matter as the heirs male only could succeed to the Forbes Baronetcy or lands of Craigievar or Fintray. My brother did not become a Roman Catholic until the 1930s when the Auld Laird pleaded hard with him not to do so. This caused the old man to leave only a life rent.

Happily now the Castle belongs to the National Trust for Scotland and is splendidly administered and looked after by this very worthy body. We have been extremely lucky at Craigievar for a number of years, in having Miss Raeburn Murray MBE as our curator. She takes a great interest in the building and is tireless in her pursuit of knowledge of the Forbeses of Craigievar. Mrs Russell, an old family retainer, is second to none as guide and worker, keeping everything in admirable condition. Improvements in the grounds have been carried out with wonderful skill by Douglas Booth. As a trustee of the estates, I shall always be glad to be associated with the legal transfer which ensured the safety of my old home in all time coming.

I must change the course of my story for a short time to explain a complicated part of the family history. In 1780, Sir William Forbes 6th Bart of Craigievar married Sarah Sempill, daughter of John 13th Lord Sempill. The Sempill family continued until the last heir male, Selkirk 15th Lord died and was succeeded by his sister Maria Janet, who became Baroness Sempill in her own right, as the peerage was an ancient Scottish one, and could descend through the female line. This lady married but had no issue, so the nearest heir was sought. This happened to be my grandfather, William Forbes 8th Bart, who was none other than the grandson of William, Forbes and Sarah Sempill. By this time sadly there was no Sempill land or residence left as they had been sold at various times, so it was merely a case of assuming the title of Lord Sempill as directed by the Lord Lyon who also instructed that my grandfather's family should adopt the hyphenated name of Forbes-Sempill. This continued for the next three generations, until my brother died without any sons. There the lines parted again and my eldest niece became Baroness Sempill in succession to the Sempill Barony, while I became 11th Baronet of Craigievar and was instructed by the Lord Lyon to drop the name of Sempill. I must say it is a great relief to have only one surname, as people often get mixed up and do not get things in their correct order. I was always brought up to be extremely grateful to my Forbes ancestors for all that we lived on from raising stock, tilling the lands and utilising game and fish as it existed on the estates. That all went with the failure of keeping the oath. I took the oath gladly, but the tragedy had already occurred. I was fortunate in acquiring the little property of Brux (meaning in Gaelic, the lythe or sheltered bank) which has been home to my wife and me for over thirty-five years with all the hard work but great enjoyment of rearing our own cattle and sheep, also tilling and harvesting the land as customs and machinery changed from the once hard work of 'forkin', leadin', biggin' rucks, and syne thrashin' the corn'.

For several years I practised medicine from Brux, putting a married assistant into my house at the surgery in Alford. I also employed a grieve and staff to carry out some farming on Brux. Unfortunately when a very excellent man left to take up a job close to the town for the benefit of his family who were now growing up I found my new grieve had spent more money than I was earning and had landed me in a financial quandary. I therefore gave up my practice with great regret

Our little Norwegian house at Brux where we fly the personal standard of Forbes of Craigievar Nova Scotia Baronetcy as of old tradition.

and rolled up my sleeves to tackle the farms in person. I dismissed three of my staff, and with the aid of my wonderful wife, tackled the job with the two remaining helpers.

As soon as I became aware of the significance of facts in Scottish history, I felt very proud that I was born on the anniversary of the Raising of the Standard on the Braes of Mar on 6 September 1715. My year was one of no great significance — 1912. My mother was much pained by a tiresome foetus which danced the Highland Fling most of the time until to her great relief, it appeard about 5 am on 6 September. My father was very bored and went out fishing, but did not even have the solace of catching anything.

By the time I was two, World War I had started. At the age of three I had certain recollections of things at home, mainly of being lifted on to a pony's back and lead about by the old coachman, who I believe was about 4 feet 10 inches and came from Yorkshire. He joined my father during soldiering days and was with us until he died. Before I was five, I was quite independent with my pony and allowed to go on the road and deliver certain messages — one I recollect very well. At that time there was an unpopular minister at Fintray, so on Sundays we attended Kirk at Kinellar a neighbouring parish about four miles away, with a long and steep brae up the final bit of road. We went in a little governess cart drawn by a Shetland pony and whoever was in the cart, got out and walked up the brae to ease the burden for the wee sheltie. At Kinellar was a much loved minister called Mr Barr. Well, it came about that one day my mother received a message that an old wifie who lived at Aikenheid, which was a croft on the top of a hill, had died and the Fintray minister had declined to conduct the service. The relatives of the deceased asked my mother to ask Mr Barr if he would do so. She agreed forthwith and wrote a letter to the good man, which was given to the five-year-old to deliver. On arriving at Kinellar Manse, I rode in at the garden gate and up to the front door where I rapped. Mr Barr himself appeared and I stated that I had a letter for him from my mother. He went away giving me a smile like a benediction and asked me to wait while he read it. When he came back, he smiled again and

The Hon Sir Ewan Forbes of Craigievar, 11th Baronet.

said, 'Tell your mother I will do what she asks. This is for you my little friend,' and he handed me a neat little wooden box of preserved fruits. I remember being allowed to have one every Sunday until the box was finished.

I recollect at about this time having a very great belief in everything the coachman told me and of course I was well instructed about harness and how a horse or pony should be properly harnessed for a gig, Brougham or any other machine — the pronunciation was Yorkshire — and my instruction was that the loop which fastened the saddle to the tail was a 'crooper'. My mother said no, it is a crupper, but I said no, Harrison said it was a 'crooper' and that must be right! At some point at the end of World War I, Harrison learned to drive the car which was a Scat. Forty mph was the top speed on the speedometer dial, but I never saw the needle approach this high figure. When we came to an incline, the driver said, 'Wᴑ-a who-a sisst' but there was no response from the horrid vehicle. We reclined in banks, hedges and ditches, and at hairpin bends we hung wavering over the edge. Every time the car was brought home, it was beautifully washed and polished accompanied by the necessary 'ss-sss' of the grooming of a horse. Experiences of being driven by my father were even more alarming and my mother always begged to be allowed to get out and walk down the hills. Once while turning at the harbour at Tayport she got a terrible fright when he nearly backed the Scat over the edge of the quay, but fortunately there was a bollard in their way. We had always been brought up to be scared about a car going up the Bandeen Brae, which was the back approach to Craigievar Castle. In August 1906 the Queen of Spain, Victoria Eugenia, with her retinue were motoring up the hill when the car stalled and started to run backwards. The sprag was let down and all personnel were ordered to get out and push. Happily no one was hurt but the incident was always brought up as a timely warning to be careful of these 'unchancy' machines.

When my father was recovering from his war wounds, he was sent to hospital in Brighton, and my mother stayed somewhere nearby so as to be able to visit him. Small outings

Madame la Baronne,

Voici le premier jour de l'An 1915.
Et nous - soldats belges convalescents, - qui jouissons de votre si large et généreuse hospitalité, et qui sommes confus de la sympathie avec laquelle vous daignez nous entourer, nous remplissons le doux devoir de vous présenter les meilleurs des vœux.

Ces vœux seront nécessairement - hélas! - d'un caractère bien différent de ceux, qu'en temps de paix nous eûmes tous le précieux privilège de pouvoir nous entre changer.
Et que faut-il vous souhaiter, Madame, sinon la fin victorieuse et incessante de nos Alliés;

Letter written by one of the Belgium wounded and signed by many
more, addressed to my mother.

que vous souhaiter de plus, que le prompt rétablissement du bonheur de votre cher foyer, qui fait la joie de vivre, et dans laquelle se complaît le monde entier.

Ce bonheur-là, Madame, nous vous le souhaitons durable et sans mélange ; nous vous le souhaitons plus parfait que jamais, et nous vous le souhaitons, enfin, Madame, humblement, il est vrai, mais du plus profond de nos cœurs.

Au service de notre vaillant Roi, Albert, nous dédaignons la mort pour la sauvegarde de notre chère Patrie, la Belgique, et pour celle des Pays belligérants, sachant de contribuer ainsi, au salut de l'Humanité entière. Mais nous caressons l'espoir de survivre aux rigueurs de cette guerre terrible, à la seule fin, Madame, de pouvoir vous faire preuve d'une reconnaissance bien vive et inébranlable, que nous inspirent vos excellents procédés, qui, influencés par un patriotisme marqué et digne, exercent sur nous d'inoubliables impressions. Ils viennent, en outre, pallier sensiblement à l'amertume de notre exil, et aux regrets que nous éprouvons tous en la pénible séparation de nos familles tant aimées, et de celle de nos chers Parents en particulier.

En vous renouvellant ces vœux de bonheur, nous vous prions, Madame, de croire à l'expression de notre respect, et de notre profonde gratitude.

Jean Hargé

Julien

Verœux

A. Berin

Fintray, le 1er Janvier 1915.

were allowed — my favourite was to a little museum which combined Natural History and many other things. Every time we went there I demanded to see and commiserate over what I called the 'bleeded ba-lamb' which was a golden eagle in a glass case standing with its talons fixed in a lamb's body at which is had been tearing with its beak and caused the flow of blood. In a big room nearby, there were a lot of Egyptian Mummies, but I was always prevented from going in there. One day, being determined to view what was on display, I devised some stratagem to delay my parents and taking to my heels charged like a dervish and completed a tour of the forbidden room before I could be caught.

During World War I, the War Office arranged to establish a hospital for Belgian wounded soldiers at Fintray House, with my mother in charge. Some of them were Walloons who did not make good contacts with our fellow Scots, but the Flemings conversed and understood the Doric well, and in turn were on a good understanding with our folk. 'Fat's the 'our (or uhr)', was a common question.

At the same time the running of the estates of Craigievar and Fintray was undertaken by my mother who was also President of the County of Aberdeen Red Cross, and in addition to other things, entertained bus loads of British walking wounded to tea every Sunday. After the war my father gave her a beautiful Italian carved oak screen for all the estate work she had undertaken. In the years following the war I was frequently dispatched on horseback carrying pails of soup — quite a balancing feat — to households smitten by 'flu' or other ailments; for those people my mother thought could not afford to pay a doctor, she would ask him to call and send her the bill.

My mother took her part in the welfare of the estates employees and tenant farmers very seriously, and had a typed list for Craigievar of about sixty holdings, and the same for Fintray, with names and addresses and a column in which she marked down the date she visited them, at least once a year and sometimes many more if there was illness. She would get a lift to the furthest point she intended to call that day and walked four or five miles home.

In her widowhood, if there was no member of the family to drive her to the Kirk, she walked from Fintray House, a mile down the west approach, then emerging at the Lodge, she climbed what is known as the Butler's Brae and then along the tree-girt road to the Kirk. Her constant companion on all days but Sunday 'Kirkin', was a little Dandie Dinmont dog. She always contrived to shut him in the house when she set out. One beautiful summer Sunday, she was half-way down the avenue when she heard the unmistakable panting of Daniel — what was she to do? — go back home or continue on her way to the Kirk? She decided to go on. On reaching the Kirk door, she explained to the elders on duty that she would tuck the Dandie under her arm and go quietly up to the loft where the Laird's pew was situated in the middle of the front, but was shut off by a door at each end. The little dog sat down quietly and all went well until the minister said 'Let us hear the Word of God . . . my reading is from Daniel!' At the sound of his name, the canine friend who was a very amiable character, wagged his tail and beat against the side of the pew, making a resounding noise, nor despite all his mistress could do, did it cease, as every few words 'Daniel' was mentioned in the text. Fortunately, Mr Cowie Farquharson was a most kindly and understanding minister. I should add that the sermon was taken from the text from the reading and Daniel was the important theme right through to the end.

After a good grounding in Scottish education, together with French and German in reading and writing, I requested to be sent to a pre-university co-ed establishment in Germany. A place was found for me in Dresden and at fifteen, I was soon on a long journey on my own. The opportunity to learn was tremendous and we had lectures for seven to eight hours daily. Life in Dresden is described later on.

ROUND THE WORLD IN A TURTLE SHELL

As a small child, I was a fashious brat, full of perpetual motion. So long as the weather was fine, my mother turned me outside and that was that, but rainy days were a problem. She solved this dilemma in a most satisfactory manner. There was a large turtle shell in the back drawingroom where she wrote her many business letters. Turning the turtle shell upside down and putting an old cushion in the bottom of it, I was told to get in and go on a voyage. This was a marvellous diversion— negotiating chairs, tables and all sorts of cabinets and ornaments as rocks, paddling with hands on the carpet, rotating at high speed round and round, and shunting from side to side like the pitching and tossing of the sea. It was an entertainment which was never boring. There was the added responsibility of not hitting the Bühl table or the Louis XVI cabinet, because anything like this was considered a disgrace, and you lost the trust which had been placed in you.

PASSING OF SEMPILL LANDS

From Statistical Account Lochwinnoch 1791-5

Family of Sempill. — But by far the most remarkable family in the ancient history of this parish was that of the Sempills, of whom a pretty full account is given by Semple and Crawfurd, continued by Robertson. I have seen a fuller and more accurate account of the family in MS., by Dr A. Crawfurd, but I cannot enter so fully into the subject as even the printed record, and shall only notice some of the most important circumstances scattered over the whole history of this family. They seem to have been vassals of the Stewarts, who at one time possessed the whole barony of Renfrew, and were progenitors of a long race of kings. In this manner, they were brought into notice at court, and made a figure in the history of the country. Walter High Steward of Scotland married Marjory; daughter of the most illustrious of Scotland's kings, Robert the Bruce, whose son, Robert Stewart, succeeded his uncle, David II., in 1371. The barony of Renfrew was called the principality, and was afterwards conferred as a separate maintenance upon the prince who was heir-apparent to the throne; and for this reason one of his titles still is "Baron of Renfrew."

Robert, the first of the Sempill family, of whom any record remains, lived in the region of Alexander II., who ascended the throne in 1214. His sons, Robert and Thomas, were great patriots, and friends of Robert the Bruce. John Sempill, the seventh of the family, was man of great talents and distinction. Amongst other public transactions in which he was engaged, he was one of the Scottish commissioners appointed to negociate with the Court of England for the liberation of James I., whom he met and congratulated at Durham when he was returning home. He was made a knight by James II. about 1430. Renfrewshire was disjoined from Lanarkshire in 1406, and Sir William Sempill, the second baronet of the family, was made Sheriff of this county, and obtained from James III. the baronies of Ellistown, Castletown, afterwards called Castle-Sempill, now Castle-Semple. Sir Thomas Sempill was killed in 1486 at Sochieburn, in the service of his sovereign, James III., who, after a fall from his horse, was treacherously put to death in the manner minutely and graphically described by Sir Walter Scott in his Tales of a Grandfather. His son, Sir John Sempill, was created Lord Sempill by James IV. in 1488. It was this Lord Sempill who built the Collegiate-Kirk of Lochwhynyeoch "to the honour of God, and of the blessed Virgin Mary, for the prosperity of his sovereign James IV., and Margaret his Queen, for the soul of Margaret Colville, his former spouse, and also for the salvation of his own soul, and that of Margaret Crichton, his present wife, and of all his predecessors and successors, and of all the faithful deceased." This wise and pious Lord, having fully appointed and richly endowed the Collegiate Kirk, died on the celebrated field of Flodden, on the 9th September 1513. The walls of the old kirk are still standing. Its whole length is 71 feet 6 inches; its breadth 24 feet 3 inches; and the height of the side wall 15 feet 6 inches. The east end of it is separated from the west by a partition, is enclosed, and still used as a burying-place by the family of Castle-Semple.

Robert Lord Sempill was called the great Lord Sempill. The family estates had been vastly increased by his father, Lord William and he being a person of a martial spirit, was engaged in many of the wars of his age. He was present at the battle of Pinkie in 1547. He adhered strictly to the interests of Queen Mary, till the murder of Darnley, after which he entered into a bond of association with other noblemen to defend the young King James. He was present with the Regent Murray at the battle of Langside, and, in consideration of his many and valuable services to the King and government, obtained from him a charter of the abbey of Paisley in 1569, upon the forfeiture of Lord Claud Hamilton. He engaged in the great feuds between the houses of Eglinton and Glencairn, or the Montgomeries and Cuninghames, with the former of which the Sempills had formed various marriage connections. These feuds lasted from 1488 till 1586. There were so many families involved in them, and so many lives lost, that is was more like a civil war, than a family quarrel. During these perilous times, Lord Sempill built the Peel on a small islet in Castle-Semple Loch. Being surrounded on all sides by water and well defended, it must have been a very safe and impregnable retreat. The foundation and a portion of the dilapidated wall still remain surrounded by a few trees and shurbs. In consequence of the extent to which the loch has been drained, the Peel now stands upon its southern margin, in the line of a high embankment, by which the land beyond it is kept comparatively dry during the summer, but which alters and hurts the appearance of this ancient place. The great Lord Sempill had three sons, Robert, who died in his lifetime, Andrew, who was the head of the Sempills of Breucheills or Bruntsheills and Millbank, and John, head of the Sempills of Beltrees. Francis Lord Sempill was the first of the family who renounced the errors of the church of Rome, to which the members of this family were long and zealously attached. Hew Lord Sempill was a Colonel in the army, and commanded the left wing of the King's forces in the battle of Culloden in 1746. He had sold Castle-Semple to Colonel Macdowell in 1727. and bought North Barr in 1741. His grandson Lord Hew Sempill was the last of the family. He had four children, of whom two are still alive; the Honourable Maria Janet Sempill, and the Honourable Sarah Sempill.

This family was the head of the clan of Sempills, and at one time possessed an extent of property, which at the present day would have produced an annual income of from L. 20,000 to L. 25,000, and therefore were properly styled "a potent and powerful family." Now the whole of that property has passed into other hands.

The Sempills of Beltrees were, in an intellectual and literary point of view, more celebrated than the great Sempill family, from which they were descended. John, the first of this family and son of the great Lord Sempill, married Mary, sister of Lord Livingstone, who was one of the maids of honour to Mary Queen of Scots. Both she and her husband were great favourites with the beautiful Queen, which was the means of promoting their wealth and worldly prosperity. His highest honour, however, was that he was the father of Sir James Sempill, his successor. Sir James was an intimate and faithful friend of Mr Andrew Melville, and therefore various important circumstances are mentioned concerning him in Dr M'Crie's Life of that celebrated individual. This intimacy is said to have occasioned the publication of the famous Basilicon Doron by James VI. Sir James Sempill, who was a friend and favourite of the King, being employed to transcribe this treatise, sent it to Mr Andrew Melville to persue. Melville taking offence at some passages which it contained, brought the subject before the synod of St Andrews, which obliged the King in self-defence, as he thought, to publish the whole work; and this step answered the pupose at least of procuring for him much admiration in England. After Melville had been decoyed to London, and cruelly and unjustly committed to the Tower by his faithless sovereign, Sir James was enabled to render him important services. He first procured for him a relaxation of his confinement and rigorous treatment, and then permission to retire to France, where he became a professor of divinity in the Protestant College of Sedan. Daniel Tilesius, a man of talent, but of Arminian principles, was his colleague, and it is supposed that, at the suggestion, and perhaps with the assistance of Melville, Sir James engaged in a controversy with him, which had the effect of preventing the spread of his opinions among the students. Provoked at this, Tilesius endeavoured to ingratiate himself with King James, by publishing a defence of the late proceedings in Scotland, and filled it with unmerited and unmeasured abuse of the Scotch Presbyterians. This was answered by Beltrees in 1622, in a book written with great ability. The style is nervous, and the satire keen, but more chastened than was necessary in answering the coarse attack of Tilesius. As intimated in the conclusion of this work, the controversy was continued, in which Sir James perhaps obtained secret assistance from Melville, and, at any rate, public and effectual aid from Calderwood, who published an elaborate work entitled "Altare Damascenum." The othere works of Beltrees were, an Answer to Tilesius's Defence of the Bishops, and the Five Articles, *Cassandra Scotiana* to *Cassander Anglicanus*, published in 1616; "Sacrilege sacredly considered," published 1619; the Packman's *Pater Noster*, a satirical poem against the Church of Rome, and probably the following production. When King James visited his native kingdom of Scotland in 1617, an oration, in the form of an allegory, welcoming his Majesty, was pronounced in the great hall of the Earl of Abercorn by a very pretty boy of nine years of age. This was William, the youngest son of the Sheriff, Sir James Sempill of Beltrees. He died in his house at the Cross of Paisley in February 1625.

His decendants seem to have retained chiefly his poetical talents, but degenerated from grave and serious subjects, to the composition of merry songs and satirical poems. His son Robert was the author of the epitaph of Habbie Simpson, the piper of Kilbarchan, and perhaps other similar productions. Francis, the next proprietor, was still more fertile in works of this kind, but, as will easily be believed, he squandered away his property, which he treated as lightly as every other subject. These light-hearted descendants of the grave and literary Sir James, when they could not rise to the composition of a poem, showed their spirit in a different way. Robert, the sixth of the family, was present at the last burning of witches in Paisley, in 1697, though to prevent this his parents had concealed his shoes, and he was obliged to go without them. It was he who died at Kilbarchan in 1789, aged 103 years. His son Robert made a little money, and retrieved the circumstances of the family, but left it all to Mr Hamilton Collins, who married his youngest sister. Mrs Campbell his eldest sister, was entirely overlooked; but her daughter married Mr Stewart, a respectable merchant in Greenock, and their son, Mr Stewart, I believe, still takes the title of Beltrees.

Family of Glen of Barr. — The second largest property in the parish is Barr, with regard to which I shall only say, it was possessed by the family of Glens above 300 years. John Glen, the first of the family, swore fealty to Edward I., King of England, in 1296, during the wars of the celebrated Sir William

Wallace; and the family became extinct in the person of Alexander Glen, in 1616.

There are, however, a few families here of the name of Glen, who are supposed to be cadets of the Glens of Barr.

The property was next possessed by the family of Hamiltons, who also sold it about half a century ago, and the only surviving branch of the family is an old maiden lady residing in the village, about eighty years of age.

Family of M'Dowall of Garthland. — The present proprietor is William M'Dowall of Garthland, Esq. whose progenitors bought Castle-Semple from Lord Hew Sempill in 1727, and ever since that period, this has been one of the most distinguished families in the country of Renfrew. The late William M'Dowall of Garthland, Esq. was frequently Member of Parliament both for the county and the Clyde district of burghs, and a very influential person at court. His memory is not merely revered in the parish, but he enjoyed so entirely the esteem of all the gentlemen of the county, that after his death they erected an elegant monument to his memory in the old Abbey Kirk of Paisley.

Land-owners. — Two of the chief land-owners in the parish have already been mentioned, Colonel Harvey of Castle-Semple, and William M'Dowall, Esq. of Garthland. The rest in the order of their valuations are, Mrs Barr; Colonel Fulton of Hartfield; Ludovic Houston of Johnstone, Esq.; William Cochran of Ladyland, Esq.; and William Patrick, Esq. W. S. The first three are resident, the following non-resident. The rest of the parish is broken down amongst a multitude of small proprietors, amounting altogether to almost 130.

EARLY YEARS

I was so much the youngest of the family, that I never had the pleasure of knowing three of my grandparents. The only one I was acquainted with was my maternal grandmother who was sweet and gentle and read her Bible every morning — one day in Latin and the next in Greek. She used to tease me by saying while pointing at my sporran, 'I know what that is, it's a sporran pocket, purse.' I remember going to visit her with my mother, I think about 1917, when there were a lot of German prisoners of war working on the farm land round about. They were mostly ploughing with a pair of horses. My mamma said, 'They will be very lonely being far away from home' and picking some snowdrops, she said, 'Go and give these to this

Ewan Forbes with tame Roe deer. (*By courtesy of Leslie Mutch.*)

man over here and say "Schneeglöckchen".' I did as I was told and he bent down and said 'Ach! danke, danke Kleines' and an enchanted smile spread across his face and great tear drops rolled down his cheeks. Shortly after that, my grandmother died — she was Welsh with a Cornish mother, which enables me to claim to be a triple distilled Celt. My brother was born in September 1893, and so was away from home before I was school age. I remember him first coming to visit us in Royal Flying Corps uniform, on a motor-bike. Five years later a sister was born with a lovely face and the sweetest disposition, so everyone agreed. Unfortunately she died of peritonitis from a burst appendix in 1910. I believe my parents were both very grief-stricken at the time. The Fintray Estate Tenantry erected a granite horse trough which is situated at the roadside just beyond the West Lodge, with a drinker for the human race at one end and a little bowl for dogs at a low level at the other end. It bears the inscription, 'Be kind to animals.' In 1905 my other sister was born and served in World War II in the WAAF, being mentioned in dispatches. When the Druminnor Estate was broken up and sold, she purchased the Castle and worked like a navvy to pull down the Simpson addition and restore the Castle to its original state. Sadly she was killed in a road accident in 1966 when on her way to dine at Brux. As a debutante she was given a London Season by our parents and I was dragged over the border to see and learn what I could of the historic buildings, museums and other things of interest. That part I enjoyed, but not much else, with the exception of being sent to study playing the harp under the expert tuition of Marie Goossens. She was a wonderful musician and full of kindness and encouragement. My mother, following in the footsteps of generations of her family, wanted one of her children to carry on the tradition and as none of the others showed any musical promise, the lot fell on me. The early twenties was a very wild and hectic time of Society nonsense and as a child, I had a very clear view from my end of the telescope, and had a pretty poor opinion of what I saw. Normality and happiness returned when we reached Aberdeenshire again.

During the summer holidays spent at Craigievar, my sister-in-law came to stay with her two enchanting children, Ann and June, who were entrusted to my care to give them riding lessons, and I took them on leading reins all round the countryside. Favourite visits were to Maggie Copland who spoiled us all. She was an elderly spinster of a famous 'Craigievar Estate family', primarily associated with the smiddy. Today, the Coplands are my very dear and staunch friends. Annie McGregor was another favourite of the children

— visits there were always associated with glasses of milk, more than half cream. Sometimes we were invited to tea with a boiled egg included. There was just one snag—Annie was a farmer having succeeded her father as tenant of Craigmill. She kept two mentally deficient 'wifies' for the parish, and amongst other duties, they were allowed to collect the eggs. They hunted round the cornyard and oh! what transport of delight when they found a carefully concealed nest at the bottom of a ruck. The eggs were all taken home with the rest, and of course, no mention made to the farmer about the nests in unusual places. When dear Annie boiled our eggs, the time

Eileen, wife of the Master of Sempill, with daughters Ann and June.

which had elapsed since they were laid was unkent to her. I got a very bad one on a certain occasion, so I stuck my bone egg spoon through the bottom of the shell and allowed the contents to disperse through the base into the egg cup. She was a very hard working and remarkable woman and had an interesting collection of antiques, such as wire 'hands' for carding wool, and a contraption called 'sleepy or lazy Maggie' which was something like a slipper open at both ends into which a mother could put her foot and, attaching a cord, rock the cradle with

Col. Stuart Chant and wife Ann, now the Lady Sempill, with
daughter Francis.

one foot, leaving her hands and other foot free to spin the yarn
with the spinning wheel.

At Muir of Fowlis, there was Jimmy Birse, well over six feet
tall with a handsome white head, a real master shopkeeper, He
was full of exciting tales about an ancestor of his who had a
merchant's business further up the Towie road, where on quite
frequent occasions, he gave the gaugers supper and a bed for
the night, while an 'all clear' signal was passed to the smugglers
coming down Donside during the darkness of night. Then with
our shalties, encouraged by frequent conversation lozenges
which they anticipated whenever they heard the rustling of the
paper bag in my pocket, we moved on to Ladymill, where
Jimmy Taylor, the finest miller in the countryside, milled our

own crop for fresh and delicious meal for our porridge. He always enjoyed a 'news', and when he was not too busy, would take time to show the youngsters all the wonders of grinding stones, chains and wonderful ways of opening up the floors and hatches. He certainly was a master. Looking at my watch, I would realise that it was high time we returned to the Castle.

There were many interesting farms on Craigievar, the special functions of which may already be forgotten by many. There was the 'Oomill' or Woolmill where the wool which had been spun by people like my mother, was taken to be woven on the looms. The next farm was the Waulkmill where the woven cloth was 'waulked' or shrunk until it was fit for the tailors to make up.

THE FUN OF CHILDHOOD

The memories of close contemporary friends and relations are always recollected with joy (if you liked them!). My two favourites were my cousins, Patrick and David Forbes of Corse, with whom much of my holiday time was spent. They came to stay at Craigievar every August, and many were the ploys we entertained ourselves with. I always had my pony, and went round and hired two more to be ready for the important arrival of my spirited cousins. We rode miles in the Castle woods and played hide and seek in the trees. I regret to say that sometimes we were taken with ideas of rodeos and lassoed and jumped on the backs of stots grazing in the grass parks. We also had a band, consisting of a melodeon, a mouth organ and a comb. Once a travelling circus passed along the road from Alford to Deeside and an elephant deposited a large dropping at the roadside near the North Knock. It appeared to be about three feet high, so we always jumped the ponies over it when coming up the road.

Life was full of fun and adventure, except when we were in trouble, which was not too infrequent. The Christmas holidays were spent at Fintray, mostly skating, and we collected as many

The author riding, with second pony on leading rein.

friends as possible including a number of able-bodied adults to play ice-hockey. I have great recollections of the late Sir Ian Forbes-Leith of Fyvie, Bart, who was a very tall man, especially when he loomed just in front of you. We also organized ice carnivals by moonlight with a few lanterns strung round. Patrick and I were a little older than David, and were positively obnoxious killing ourselves with laughter, when David and his truly delightful mother fell through the thin area of ice on one occasion.

The Grants of Monymusk were all very old friends and the boys had a splendid game of cutting turf into divots and battering each other with them — I enjoyed it very much. One time, Francis Grant came to stay with me at Fintray, and we found mischief to do — I think he was six and I was seven. He dared me to drop as large a stone as would go into the top of the lum down to the fire that was burning below. There was a hideous clatter and a wifie's voice shouted up, 'Get oot o' that ye little vratch or I'll . . .' We slid down the slates tearing our breeks, and never stopped running until we reached the kennels half a mile away.

The Crombies at Goval were very good and kind neighbours and always had chocolate biscuits for tea, which was something never seen at Fintray, although the provision of home baking was enormous.

I always found being dressed up for social occasions was a great bore, or even conforming to endless apparently senseless conversation. When people came to call — out of the blue — I ran at high speed to the old schoolroom window which was about 12 feet off the ground, then with a judicious jump, I landed on the back lawn and tore like fury until I was out of sight and hearing, so that I could say with truth, 'I never heard you call me.'

Nothing was greater fun than escaping to the Home Farm at Fintray, where several families of hardy youngsters lived. I organised athletics in which we all competed, and prizes were sticks of rock acquired by bartering empty ale bottles gathered by beachcombing on the river sandbank or Silver Strand (Fion Traigh) from which Fintray takes its name. One bottle cost a penny and two sticks of rock could be bought against this plunder. I taught a lot of the youngster to ride and drive, and in the winter, we were able to muster two-horse-drawn sleighs and have some splendid runs on a Saturday.

One ploy was very highly organised, and we all drilled for action stations to make war on rats in the two large granaries. Wearing rubber soles if possible, we crept up the long outside stair, then rushed in with sticks waving. Wee Willie Forbes was always stationed at the fan, which he turned after the first attack, and a whole lot more rats came out. Lastly we looked at the bags filled with grain and if we saw any movement, we seized the bodies and gripped them until all struggles ceased. No one was ever bitten!

Random childhood memories include watching the Victory Parade in the Mall, also viewing Princess Mary's wedding procession from Buckingham Palace and back up the Mall again from a house in Carlton House Terrace where friends of my mother stayed. I remember being threatened with immediate annihilation if I uttered one word.

When I was thirteen, I had a very lucky experience of being asked during my winter holidays, to spend the time with my Uncle Charlie, who was a brother of my mother and married to a wife with quite a fortune. He rented a flat in a villa at St Moritz. There I had the chance to learn to ski, also to make a study of figure skating. I had already learned to skate at home, so the elimentary part was already overcome. I took my two preliminary tests at the Club de Patineurs de Lausanne. As my behaviour passed muster, I was asked back next year and again had a lot of fun. I made great friends with the Cartier family and wrote to my mother to say that I had met these very nice people, whom I understood had a jewellers' shoppie in London — their parents I think were in USA at the time. I persuaded one of them to join me in a two-man bob venture. We won a race and were much cheered. Later on there was an important race on the Bob Run, but ten Swiss Francs (about 8s.) was required to hire a horse-drawn sleigh to pull our bobsleigh and ourselves from the bottom to the top of the run, and I didn't have that large sum. Uncle Charlie said, 'Aren't you going to try the open international race?' I explained my financial difficulty, whereupon ten francs were put at my disposal. It was a big competition and we ended up second, much to our delight. All of a sudden, a fearful noise started up and the leading bobsleigh was turned upside down, revealing 300 lbs of lead screwed into the bottom. Immediate disqualification resulted and Cartier and Forbes emerged victorious. Another form of winter sport fired my imagination. There were ski-joring races held on the frozen and snow covered lake below St Moritz, where chaps on skis were pulled individually as they drove their horses in competition. This appealed to me very much, so I put it into practice at home, but of course I never had anyone to race. It was very exciting none-the-less, as I tore along the roads at home which were usually very ice-bound, even with the modest amount of traffic of 1926. A fresh

fall of snow always made things safer, as one had to be very
wary not to overtake the horse going down steep braes, also it
was only with vigorous stemming that one could exert sufficient
pull to stop the equine friend. When I did not have the
company of my cousins, or my friends at the Fintray Home
Farm, I was often very lonely, but I had a very warm
understanding with all the horses and ponies. Apart from
looking after them, I often lay down beside them or sat on their
backs facing the rear and put my head on their warm
comforting rumps. I had a special friend at Craigievar in the
form of a mummified head which my father had picked up in
the desert beside Wadi Halfa. He had startling red hair and
almost a complete dentition of very strong teeth. When you
moved the head, there was lots of rattling sounds caused by the
many little bones in the air sinuses. I called him the 'mannie'
and felt he was really a very sincere friend. He resided in the
Piper's Gallery at Craigievar. One day, unbeknown to me, my
mother had him buried with Christian rites, which probably
may have troubled his soul, as I felt he was a Muslem. She felt
that it was indecent for him not to be buried and later
explained this to my childish and enquiring mind. Many years
later when the British Medical Association met in Aberdeen
just before World War II, my mother put forward her name as
a willing hostess to take Members, especially from abroad, to
stay for the Conference. Amongst others, we had Dr and Mrs
Hofmeyer from South Africa. She asked them to take back
with them what was hitherto known as an Afrikans Bible,
which had been brought to Scotland by my father when he
fought in the wretched South African War. There were names
written in the bible, and my mother was most concerened that
it sould be returned to its rightful owners. The Hofmeyers were
endeavouring to trace the family when I last heard, but of
course all normality was upset by the war. They very kindly
sent us food parcels which were much appreciated.

THE ANNUAL SUMMER FLITTING

At the beginning of August every year, the whole household set out from Fintray in a carefully devised plan to arrive at Craigievar by an exciting and varied means of transport. In the vanguard went the head housemaid, two days in advance, on her bicycle. This would give her time to make up all the beds with the overseer's wife, who was caretaker of the Castle in winter. At 9 am on 'D' day, my mother driving a Shetland pony in a governess cart, and my sister driving another wee shalt in a flat cairtie and myself mounted on a riding pony, set on our way. We always put in at the stables at House of Monymusk, where the good coachman attended to our ponies, while we had lunch with that most hospitable Lady, the wife of Sir Arthur Grant. After lunch, we continued on our journey. Meantime, the milk cow with the cook and a certain amount of baggage, set off in a small hired cattle float. You might think the cook was riding shotgun, but the whole timing was calculated so that food could be prepared for the many who would arrive in due course. The cook undoubtedly was the most important individual there. Later in the day, the chauffeur drove the large Siddely Deasy with all the rest of the staff except the butler, who risked his life, with my father driving an Essex and bringing varied bits of table silver and the rest of the luggage. By 7.30 pm, the whole move had been completed, thanks to the flair for planning possessed by my mother. I should not forget to add, that the milk cow was very well milked by the overseer's wife, who had a great rapport with all animals.

During one of these glorious summer holidays, my precious pony developed stifles, for which the vet prescribed a quart of linseed oil mixed half and half with treacle, twice a day. I held her head up while the overseer poured the mixture down her throat. Unfortunately, he was frightened of horses, which my little mare realised after one dose. Next time I saw her rolling her eyes with a very wicked expression and as the poor man poured the dose down her throat, she closed her gullet and

Flitting from Craigievar to Fintray, 1919; left to right Margaret Forbes-Sempill, the Lady Sempill, and the author.

The author on Tommy.

blew the lot over him. He seemed to be doomed to stickiness, as
during the summer months, various swarms of bees chose their
residences in the roof of the Castle. A trap door was made for
access to the honey above a large space known as the long
room. Old hip baths, berry pans and basins were prepared to
receive an enormous weight of honey. On one occasion the
butler's bedroom ceiling, situated immediately below the
square tower was weighed down and drooped in a very
dangerous manner. He was hurried away to other quarters, as
his bed was menaced by honey and bees. As soon as the family
had flitted to the house at Fintray, the joiner cut the ceiling
and the portly figure of the overseer, well covered in a straw
hat and veils all around, made his entry through the aperture,
and lo there came forth sweetness, which ran in a sticky
cascade down his jacket, waistcoat and right down his breeks,
until he could touch nothing without becoming cemented to
the spot. His wife gave me a blood-curdling description of her
adventures in removing his garments.

My pony with the stifles, abandoned herself happily and willingly to Mrs Copland, who spoke to her in the approved manner and poured down the linseed and treacle without spilling a drop over either of us.

As will be known to all visitors at Craigievar, there is only one door and as the ground floor windows will only open about 6 inches. As a youngster I would rather do anything than get entangled with high-society people who came to kill time and landed conveniently at tea time, as my mother was well-known for her remarkable ability of organising teas for over forty people when no one was expected at all, I was thin enough to wriggle through the kitchen windows and make my escape.

When no strangers were about, I caught a number of bumble bees and put them in a match box, then going to the outside wall of the kitchen where a hole had been bored through the wall 3 inches diameter and 3 feet long, opening into a cupboard, I called, 'Hoo hoo,' and blew the bumble bees down the pipe. I didn't get an oatcake piece for my pony or myself for two days.

No account of life at Craigievar would be complete without including that wise and wonderful character known as Postie Lawson. He was like a magnet which drew many people of different interests to visit him. He had been a postman with a great inventive genius which he put to good work in many practical ways. One was a little horse-drawn wagon with windows all round a shelf in front of the driving seat, surrounded by a little flange to keep the letters from sliding off. Immediately in front of him was an opening through which the reins were passed, so the horse could be driven all the time from the shelter at the side of the sorting shelf. He could slide the window open and pass the letters out to their addressees. Thus no snow or rain wet him or his mail. He dug a lade which he diverted from the burn and constructed a water wheel to connect up with various wires, that achieved many things. He ploughed by water power, made his own electricity, arranged an old-fashioned plumping churn for his wife to make butter, by merely connecting some driving shafts. He had a so-called motor car, made out of wood, with something

Postie Lawson with his steam car, the Craigievar Express.

inside called a quad, which I think was a tricycle with an extra wheel. I never saw it in working order. Undoubtedly his claim to fame was that he made the first steam car in the North of Scotland. I wanted to know how he got the parts for it. He said its fire box and boiler came off a little boatie that 'gied' on the Thames. My brother received a gift of this wonderful machine after Postie's death and it was his delight to drive famous airmen about, stoking up the fire and making the black reek and smuts blow back all over them. My illustration will give my reader some idea what it was like.

Postie made many little gadgets with arms and legs that whirled in the wind. He also collected grandfather clocks and a great number of wag-at-the-wa' models with ornate paintings. If he went into a secondhand shop, he invariably became overcome by the longing to acquire some particular object. One day I went along to visit him, and found him outside. 'Come in and see my new "umman".' 'Fitna new umman?' I said. 'Come intil the barn or ye see', and there lying on the floor was a statue on its back with an arm severed at the shoulder. The detached portion was holding a blazing torch. 'She cam fae a mansion hoose about Dyce.' She was obviously some mythological character, bearing a light. Postie suddenly exclaimed looking at the gaping hole in the shoulder — 'I was gaun to stick on her airm, but it took five pails fill o' cement tae fill her briest.' Mrs Lawson said, 'Faur are ye gaun to pit her?' 'In the recess in the room.' 'Ye canna, the knock's there.' 'We'll shift the knock.' 'Well if she's comin' in, I'm gaun oot, sae ye choose atween the twa o's.' Being a sensible man, he chose his wife. The premises were completed with photographic studio with rustic seats and large tree stumps. upon which languid Victorian figures leaned to have their likenesses recorded by the camera.

HISTORY LEARNED FROM JUNK ROOMS

There were two sort of junk rooms at Fintray in the more or less unused part of the large house, which consisted of twenty bedrooms and eight living rooms. One was the box room used for this purpose and also full of cases of stuffed birds, much frowned upon as Victoriana. Nevertheless, they were beautifully done by an expert taxidermist. All game birds were in pairs in glass cases to fit their natural size. With these I was well acquainted. There was one very large case, about five to six feet high and about six feet long, which was filled by a tree with many branches and an enormous collection of song birds. Equipping myself with 'Morris's *British Birds* from the library downstairs, I made a close study of these lovely creatures, and there for the first time, discovered which was the cuckoo! There was an enchanting picture of the Falls of Schaffhausen, near the source of the Rhine, and a lot of pictures of German shooting parties with elaborate sporting gear and in every one my grandfather was included. Here I must digress to explain the reason for this. My great-grandfather, it will be remembered, was a second son, but on the death of his brother — Sir Arthur 6th Bart — he succeeded to the family estates as well as Corse, which had already been left to him by his father. As he had been working for the East India Company, like all other Nabobs, he had made a lot of money. When he succeeded his brother in 1823, he came home a very wealthy man. In May 1824, he married Charlotte Elizabeth, daughter of General the 18th Lord Forbes, but no son was born until 1836. In 1846, Sir John died and was succeeded by his ten-year-old son, William. William was far to young to have any idea of estate administration or the prudent spending of money. He joined the Coldstream Guards, and took his own piper and a considerable number of barrels of whisky to the Crimea, where he entertained his brother officers most liberally, holding ceilidhs and festivities whenever possible. When the Crimean War was over, he bought the billiard table, which was used at Donnybrook camp by most of the British Officers, and had it shipped home to Aberdeen. I don't recollect that the table cost very much, but the freight was £100. The Crimean medal was painted on the end of the table, while the ribbon was painted right round the side. Spending was continued on a lavish scale, and in the late 1850s, this dashing Heilanman married his pretty kinswoman Caroline Louisa Forbes, daughter of Sir Charles Forbes of Newe, Bart. Unfortunately, he was often away from home on various ploys and neglected his lovely young wife, who caused time to pass more amusingly with a young officer called Captain Gibbard. Alas, he divorced her, saying that the little daughter she bore was not his. Subsequent years, showed up the Craigievar family likeness most clearly, and she became the most loved of all our relations. Her tombstone is inscribed 'loving and beloved'. My grandfather then married Frances Abercromby daughter of Sir Robert Abercromby of Birkenbog Bart and Forglen, by whom he had a large family. The spending went wildly on, until my father and some other members of the family banished him to the Black Forest with a pittance to live on. He was full of fun and energy, and becaue fêted by kindly residents of the Black Forest, to whose parties he was in constant demand. Eventually he earned his reprieve and was allowed home to live his life 'amon his ain fowk' at Craigievar, where he was a kenspeckle figure in his kilt. He was often entertained by Queen Victoria, for whom he used to perform his Highland dances, and I believe, was allowed the privilege of smoking his pipe in her presence. He insisted upon the family learning to become skilled Highland dancers, and made them practise extra tricky steps, like going down on one knee in the rocking step. I was much interested to learn that he collected various musical instruments, which he taught himself to play, also that he took pains to learn German dialects, which I had been doing for some time, and never knew that any of my progenitors had been taken with the same ideas, as I would myself.

The box room also contained many other things of interest, like beautifully painted meerschaum pipes of elaborate patterns, dog collars with an over-collar of brass with double rows of spikes to protect your own dog from being guzzled round the neck. There was an old tobacco cutter, rather like a neep chopper, with which I had a yearly job to cut up 2 cwt of soap bars, from the Southern Drysalteries in Glasgow, into squares for household use. No such niceties as soap powder existed in those days. The squares all had to be built up in arches, to allow the air to circulate freely to dry the soap firmly and enabled it to last much longer. There was also a fire engine, painted red which ran on three wheels, and had a hose and nozzle attached, also a pump so that two people could attack a blaze on a modest scale. My father decided that the house should have a portable fire escape, and decided on one with a cord rolled on a drum and a substantial hook to fasten it to a windowsill. The escaping body then fastened the rope round his torso and descended from the top window. I volunteered to try it out, and all went well, except that I forgot to make allowance for the 8 foot high windows on the way down, and gave a shove off from the wall at one of the windows, and of course, broke a pane of glass. Happily for me no scolding ensued.

Sadly, Fintray House was demolished at the end of the war, and there was no room to have the many things it contained. What pleasure it would have given me to have gifted some of these things I have described, to a rural museum or some place where other youngsters could have learned as I did, from simply looking and benefiting from what I saw. Unfortunately they were not mine to give, and were dispersed during the war while I was working in hospital, and had no time to investigate anything else. The other room, not often used, was a billiard room with the famous table from the Crimean War. My grandfather turned its walls into a history of this campaign and the part played particularly by the Coldstream Guards, and all their variety of winter uniforms with fur-lined jackets and boots. Turkish sabres and knives were hung round the walls. There were also some depressing scenes, like the retreat from Inkermann, with many wounded depicted. The landing of the British Fleet at Sebastapol involved an amazing mass of craft from battleships down to minute litte boats of all descriptions. I certainly took in more information that I ever learned from my history books.

HOLIDAYS AT FOCHABERS

When I was about six or seven, it was a great treat to visit my aunt and her husband, who was Commissioner to the Dukes of Richmond and Gordon. He had ten factors working under him on the Duke's vast estates from Enzie to Glenmore and up Glenlivet. The organisation was tremendous. There were all the beautiful things like the lake at Gordon Castle with the lovely water lilies and the ice house cut far into the bank, where all the blocks of ice were stored to keep the household going all summer. The famous Duchess Tree was a delight which kept me and other youngsters playing for hours. How glad I am that a member of our Aberdeen Scottish Country Dance Society Branch has created a magnificent dance called The Duchess Tree, to Scott's Skinner's enthralling music. Then there was the miracle of peaches and nectarines growing in the open on the garden walls. My uncle was a famous scholar and ornithologist and received an LLD at Aberdeen University. I am very fortunate in being left many of his books, including Jamieson's *Dictionaries of the Scottish Language,* Douglas's *Peerages,* and *Baronage of Scotland.* When this much loved pair set out on a journey in the old Minerva, Dr Muirhead would be sitting waiting patiently for about an hour, and his wife never appeared. He said to the chauffeur, 'I'll just go and have a bath.' Shortly afterwards, his wife would arrive and demand to know, 'Where is Dr Muirhead?' I think this was his own quiet way of protesting about some of these long waits. They never quarrelled and no angry word was ever spoken, which made it such a paradise to holiday in. Speybank was the name of the house near Fochabers, and it was surrounded by wonderful gardens crammed with flowers, shrubs and fruit trees, always heavy with the scent of lovely roses and many beautiful flowers and a constant working of bees, which made the air drowsy. My aunt kept tame pigeons as was done in doo' cots in the old days to replenish the larder in a bygone age. Their roucoucouller added to the calming of the general atmosphere, and the dear lady herself always came out and

cooed to them. The heavily scented air always reminded me of
Lady Nairn's song about 'The Auld Hoose' and 'Mony tender
memories did they sweet flooers reca!' God was in his heaven,
and all our paths were peace!

In August, these two dear people went up to Glenlivet for
the Commissioner's holiday, where he shot grouse with a few
old friends. It was always walking up, and by the time the
morning was over, they were very ready for their dram and
their piece. This was conveyed to an agreed rendezvous by an
old retainer with a shaltie and panniers to collect the bag and
hand out the refreshments. At the agreed spot, the guns espied
the shaltie but did not find the pony man at first, but as it was
a very hot day, he was found reclining in the heather, but wae's
me, the bottle of whisky was lying in the heather — empty. One
of the guests present said my uncle emitted a low whistling
sound. Fortunately the burn was near by and the success of the
day made up for the empty bottle, but no risks were run in
future.

DRESDEN 1928-9

On arrival in Dresden, I was informed that this was the evening
of the week when the students were having their weekly outing
and on this occasion, it was a magnificent production of one of
Schiller's plays. I was very tired after my long journey, but
determined not to miss anything, so I listened with great intent
to grasp every word. On normal occasions we were instructed
to read the play first. When our evening out was an opera, we
studied the story, but principally the music, so as to become
well acquainted with the different arias and themes. We had a
very inspiring lecturer on this subject, who, having explained a
certain theme, sat down at the piano and played it, then
adjusting his pince-nez, picked on a member of the class to
hum the music and be sure to get it right. When the night of
the opera came, our enjoyment was greatly enhanced by this
means. We spent many hours of study on Wagner's *Ring der*

Nibelungen from the clump of the giants 'Riesenmotif' to the enchanting 'Waldweben' the spider's web in the forest glistening with the sparkle of drops of dew. There were only a few students who were not German, so we did not seem to have any special classes for language, grammar etc., but were corrected when we wrote about literature, history and architecture. Speaking the language constantly was the great advantage. I had a special study following on Marie Goosens harp lessons. Herr Gottschalk who was principal harpist at the opera, came every week to give me several hours of teaching. He always came to the little college and I shared fitting in my lessons with others studing different instruments as time would allow. I always remember my harp master well clad in a very warm black overcoat, a fur hat and black velvet lug coverings which clipped on individually like tea-cosies. The winter of 1928–9 was exceptionally cold and I recall the navigation of the Elbe was completely at a standstill. On the other hand, traffic moved about freely on the frozen river. Lectures were postponed till evening so that we could go and skate on sports grounds flooded for this purpose, and also for a game known as Eis-schiessen, played with blocks of wood and very reminicent of curling—'but it wisna sic a roarin' game'. It seemed to be the entertainment of old men.

At week-ends, all those with the will and the energy, boarded a bus and went to the Sächische Schweiz or towards the Bohemian Forest. The ski-ing was mostly of the Langlauf nature with very exciting tours through the vast forests. Although the youngest of the party, I was put in charge of leading these expeditions as I had more general experience of ski-ing in Switzerland and at home. I became nicknamed the Wichtel Männchen. There were occasional signs set up in the forest indicated how many kilometres to such-and-such a hamlet. One day when we were all beginning to feel very hungry after a 5 am start, a cosy little inn appeared as we reached a clearing in the trees. We entered with alacrity and had a splendid lunch set before us. I do not recollect the menu but red cabbage with apple was very appetising and the beer excellent. The enchanting notes of the Zitter player entranced us so that we felt loath to leave.

At that time, food still seemed to be very short in Germany, as she took a long time to recover from the blockade of World War I, and then was beset by fantastic inflation. I remember in college, we had a little meat once a week, an egg once a week, and some milk in our tea on Sundays only, and butter did not exist — jam was made of mangolds, but all the German students were most generous and shared anything special they might have got from home with the strangers within their gates. Nothing was spared on education, but food was very poor. When I came home, I had a lot of cavities in my teeth.

My mother came out to see me at Easter 1929, and we had a most enjoyable trip to Prague where we saw the Castle and all the wonderful buildings, also the beautiful bridges over the Moldau. In a few days we moved on to Vienna where, of course, we visited the Hofburg and Schönbrunn and the fabulous picture galleries, then doing a bit of nosing around, I found out where Hof Reitschule was situated and made a cautious approach to be allowed to enter the stables where at that time, thirty-two stallions of the famous Lipizzaner breed were stabled. I made friends with the grooms and was allowed a number of privileges. I learned about the techniques of the 'Levade', 'Capriole', 'Piaffe' and a number of other things. There was a most agreeable arrangement between the Opera and the Hof Reitschule, when the State Opera had a production which required horses on the stage — gorgeous white stallions appeared with great decorum and impeccable manners. To reciprocate this friendly act, about a dozen members of the Vienna Philharmonic Orchestra would appear in the minstrels gallery in the beautiful Imperial Riding School and play on a Sunday morning for a demonstration of dancing and other skills performed by the Lipizzaner stallions with their riders in the traditional Spanish uniforms with their bi-corn hats. To anyone who has not already done so, I would recommend reading Colonel Alois Podjasky's book about these famous white horses which he evacuated from Vienna to a safe country retreat during World War II. This was devised with great stealth against the Nazi Command. To turn back in time to this Easter Holiday in 1929, there was a minor earthquake while we were in Vienna, but as far as I know, no real damage done. We were told that on the Saturday evening, there was a celebration of the Resurrection in the famous St Stephen's Cathedral. We joined in and there was such a press at the great door, that I found I was lifted off my feet and borne in with many others by the sheer weight of the crowd. The organ music was glorious.

We stayed at the Hotel Meissel Und Schaden where we duly wrote under nationality 'Schottisch'. There was great delight recorded by the hotel staff, who recollected with great pleasure, the visit of 'eine wunderbare Schottische Dame' who was none other than our revered neighbour, Lady Aberdeen of 'We Twa' fame who had been attending a conference.

One of my mother's chief delights were the paintings by Velázquez of all the little Archdukes and Archduchesses of the Hapsburg family, painted in the very elaborate clothing of the time and looking like miniature adults.

One more delight was to come before we left Vienna, a visit to the opera where we heard *Tannhäuser* with Friedrich Schorr as a visiting singer from the Berlin State Opera.

Once more heading south on the train, we arrived in Budapest where we had bedrooms with balconies overhanging the Danube. Fortunately, many people could speak German, so we were able to find out much that would otherwise have passed us by. At that time Hungary was still a kingdom without a king. Admiral Horthey was the Head of State. I never quite fathomed why Lord Rothermere had so much to do with the Hungarian parliament. The usher who showed us round wouldn't stop speaking about him. There were some very exotic restaurants with Zigeuner Musik, sometimes played a bit too far down your neck so as to come between you and your partner. One of the places which interested me most was a wonderful museum, which gave a complete picture of agricultural activity and ways of tillage, crop growing, harvesting and a very comprehensive explanation of life in the vast plains of Hungary. Alas, this electrifying fortnight came to an end and a return to Dresden for the summer term was necessary. All classes were continued with some extra summer outings. A journey by river steamer on the Elbe to Meissen was one of great interest. Fortunately I knew a certain amount about the wonderful porcelain, as my family had inherited a beautiful collection, left to my great-great-great-grandfather by his life-long friend Sir Andrew Mitchell. Sir Andrew had been British Ambassador to the Court of Frederick the Great. Frederick took such a liking to the old man that he made him accompany him even when he was on a journey or when campaigning. On one occasion when the King of Prussia was on a visit to the Saxon Court, he took a great interest in the Meissen porcelain factory. So did Sir Andrew Mitchell, who purchased an enormous quantity of figurines, also dinner and tea services and a cabinet covered in plaques of quaint beautifully painted porcelain. The great secret of the Meissen Factory was that Friedrich Böttger discovered the ancient Chinese formula for making fine porcelain hitherto unknown in Europe. Early in 1700 he started the manufacture of this porcelain in Meissen. The process of making this china was to fashion the china clay, then bake it followed by glazing. Afterwards all the designs are hand painted by artists and then lightly glazed over the whole article. We spent the day in the factory to learn the process thoroughly. Sir Andrew Mitchell was the only son of the minister of St Giles and ultimately bought the estate of Thainstone on the Don. He received the Knighthood of the Order of the Bath and was painted by Reynolds. He was specially chosen by the British Government to keep Frederick the Great active against France to take the pressure off the English forces. He also conducted a very successful campaign against the Holy Roman Empire. Sir Andrew was with him during this occasion, and after the Battle of Rosbach which was a great victory for Frederick, the troops were resting in their camp when they suddenly burst into singing as with one voice, the Lutheran Hymn, 'Now thank we all our God'. It was the first time a battle had been won against the Holy Roman Empire.

Another most interesting outing was to Moritzburg which was the hunting lodge of Augustus the Strong. He was a very tall and powerfully built man and it is related that he used to

stand on the edge of one of the terraces at Moritzburg and hold
two trumpeters by the back of their uniforms while they blew a
salute. He had over one hundred mistresses and is said to have
fathered over one thousand children. One I believe became a
ballet dancer and was the mother of the writer George Sands,
Chopin's paramour. The Hunting Lodge was surrounded by a
massive swamp on one side. I thought I heard sheep bleating
but it turned out to be a special kind of frog. Behind the lodge
was a forest abounding with wild boar. On entering the large
cental hall of the building, I was amazed to see the walls hung
with stags' heads, all Imperial or Royal heads of red deer —
there must have been hundreds. In one place of honour was a
sixty-six pointer which had been gifted to the King of Saxony
by the contemporary Elector of Brandenburg. It had originally
been picked up dead in the forest of Brandenburg, probably
discovered after a mortal combat with another stag. Of course,
the heads were so much larger than those we have at home in
Scotland, because of the tremendous quantity of lime in the
soil. To me it was a day I shall never forget. There were many
beautiful buildings in Dresden — the opera house in the middle
of a large cobbled platz. Here many famous composers had
conducted, Carl Maria von Weber about 1820 and many
more.

The Zwinger Palais was a delightful and most unusual
German Rococo wall round an open space with a pavilion at
one end. One could walk within the walls or on a sort of
promenade deck round the top. I remember one summer
evening just as darkness fell, attending a real promenade
concert. It was *Haffner's Serenade* by Mozart, composed
especially to celebrate the wedding of the daughter of Haffner,
who was the Burgomaster of Salzburg. The time was planned
for the beginning of the concert for the lights to go on for the
orchestra in the pavilion and other very artistic lighting round
the Rococo Walls. The audience could move freely all the
time.

Then there was the Brüllische Terrasse, which Napoleon
had named the eighth wonder of the World. The Hofkirche
was a very beautiful building. I remember visiting the Russian

Church to hear the remarkable singing of the Greek Orthodox
Religion. I normally attended the Lutheran Church for
Sunday praise, but occasionally went to the American Embassy
Church as there was no Scots Kirk and the American Consul
carried out any diplomatic requirements for British subjects.

PLEA TO STUDY MEDICINE

Having finished my schooling, my heart was set on studying
medicine, so I approached my father about his willingness to
pay my fees at the University of Aberdeen. I felt that my
reports from my various institutions of study proved that I had
done my work well and had earned my right to choose a career
for myself. I was wounded to the core when I met with a frank
refusal to be bothered paying out anything more on me. There
was no need for it and plenty of work for me to do at home, for
which I would receive my keep. I could plant trees, fence and
was able to help in all estate work. I could also market garden
produce and do all driving jobs needed. I had no hope of ever
achieving a life of my own. I knew that to argue against this
was quite useless, so I made up my mind to earn £1000 in my
spare time, which I reckoned would cover my expenses up to
graduation. The BBC was a source of bits of income, and
anything that turned up, down to beach-combing on the river
bank. I still found time to do a lot of dancing for raising
charity funds. In 1933, I had a wonderful chance to study at
the University of Munich under Dr Seif, who was professor of
Adlerian Psychology. This was due to the great kindness of the
American writer Phyllis Bottime who was married to a Forbes
relative, and they had a house in Munich, where they invited
me to be their guest during this course of study.

It all coincided with the German elections, when the
Hindenburg Party came to power, and that evil genius Hitler
climbed on the band wagon in the wake of old Field Marshal
Hindenburg. I only knew one Hitler supporter when I was
there, and the enthusiasm of the Bavarians was all for their

own party the 'Bayrische Volkspartei'. There were frequent
skirmishes in the streets between the brown shirts and the
communists, and within a week of the election results, revealed
the planning of the curtailment of freedom, and the
imprisonment of good and influential people, who were held
for weeks and months without any charges being made against
them. I was friendly with a number of international students
and before the elections took place, we went together in a
group for a lark one evening, to the Exhibition Park where
Hitler was going to speak. For the first time I heard him
screaming over the public address system, 'In den letzten
vierzehn Yahren haben wir nur knechtschaft gehabt' (in the
last fourteen years, we have had only thirldom), then at every
focal point, there were people directing, shouting of Zieg Heil!
Zieg Heil! The main building could not contain the whole
crowd, so many stood outside in the deep but well trampled
snow, while others got into auxiliary buildings. One very large
Canadian in our group leaned against some glass panes, which
promptly fell in and we all walked through. We still thought it
was all a joke. Massed bands would strike up in the very frosty
air, then there would be dead silence. Suddenly a brown-shirt
would rush across an open space shouting, 'Der Hitler kommt',
then several others were organised to shout, 'Where? where?
where?,' followed by more martial music, and further shouting
that Hitler was about to appear. All hysterical dramatisation.

   The great opportunity of learning was once again realised.
The Forbeses, were like fairy godparents to me, and at
different times to many more young people, some of them very
famous in after years, like Ivor Novello and Ian Fleming. Life
in their household was tremendously interesting, where people
of literary and musical talent were always meeting. Phyllis was
a very old friend of Dorothy Thompson, the American
journalist, who had crossed swords with Hitler in the 1920s.
She was full of amusing anecdotes. We had a very fine dinner
in a famous Munich restaurant, during which Dorothy
explained that she had been up to Berlin to see what was going
on. Hitler was speaking in the Sportz Palast, and every time the
Zeig Heil shout was initiated, there was an extraordinary

amount of background noise. She immediately set out to
investigate the cause, so she climbed up into the rafters and
discovered a number of men engaged in rolling empty beer
barrels in the roof on a given signal. How great was the
applause for the Fuhrer!! She also told us about her husband
Sinclair Lewis, also a writer, when they lived in California
where everything grew and flourished faultlessly. One day she
met him going out of the house and said, 'Where are you
going, Sinclair?' 'I'm goin' out to kick a rose!'

Dr Seif had a wonderful gift of humour. He used to say that
life without humour is like a soup without salt. His little
waiting room had a picture of a milk jug filled to the brim with
milk, and two frogs. The story annexed was that overnight the
two frogs fell in. One said, 'Weh und Ach!' gave up the struggle
and drowned. The other frog said, 'Come on and try,' and
paddled hard all night. In the morning he emerged on the top
with the caption, 'Morgan, Festes Land! Butter!' (in the
morning, solid land! Butter!). How useful my training with Dr
Seif proved to me in general practice.

RURAL CEILIDHS

As autumn days hastened the early approach of dusk, at the
hint o'hairst and stacks safely thackit, I used to be invited
round to different farms for my tea and everyone who played a
musical instrument, even the piano with one finger, was roped
into an enthusiastic evening of richt Scots tunes. My
contribution was with a melodeon slung on my back while I
rode to the appointed farm on my shalt, which was
comfortably stabled during the evening's celebrations.
Sometimes we had the old family governess, Miss Greig, to
stay, and she was a very good pianist — she was also an able
cyclist and pedalled blithely to the site of the entertainment.
Drumriach near the Kirk at Leochel-Cushnie was a favourite
venue, where old Tibbie Garioch played Orange and Blue on
the piano with one finger and her brother John joined by

Sir John Forbes, 9th Bart of Craigievar and 18th Lord Sempill, with
his wife, in Coronation Robes 1910.

several neighbour farmers, played the fiddle. What glorious evenings we had making our own entertainment.

Some time about the end of the 1920s, I had entered the Abedeen Music Festival in the Scots Verse speaking session and was lucky enough to win it with 'The Braw Lass'. Shortly after that, I was invited by Beltona to make a number of records for them of Charles Murray's poems, so off I went to London, where they roped me in for some harp solos at the same time. With the money earned, I bought a piano-accordion which helped to contribute to our musical evenings.

There was one more period of study for me to complete, this time in Paris. Lectures at the Sorbonne were fine, but I found that the curriculum was very lax and that we did not get the chance to work nearly hard enough, as had been the case in Dresden. Of course, there were many beautiful things and places to see, and some lovely stage productions. At the Malmaison there is a picture by Winterhalter of the Empress Eugenie, the wife of Napoleon III surrounded by her ladies in waiting. I was enchanted by the exact recreation of the scene on the stage of the Theatre Pigalle by Sacha Guitry. The picture was frozen in action on the stage inside a frame and suddenly it all came to life and there was singing, dancing and conversation, then with great skill, every actress melted into her original posture and we were once again viewing Winterhalter's delightful painting.

I did continue my harp studies with the principal harpist from the opera, but on the whole, I was quite glad when my time in Paris was finished, It was spring once again, and my mother joined me before taking her annual sketching holiday, but before she set off on her own, we went to Oberammergau and saw the final rehearsal of the Passion Play before the 1930 production was open to the public. I shall never forget the very moving experience at the time of the crucifixion. The stage which was in the open air, became cloaked over with dark purple clouds — it is now over fifty years ago but I recollect it very clearly. While we stayed there, the gentians, wild primulas and auriculas made the meadowland and the rocks enchanting. I have a picture in our bedroom which was painted by an artist friend of my favourite aunt, looking from Oberammergau to Unter-Ammergau, and every morning when we wake up, my wife and I look at this lovely scene.

PHYLLIS AND ERNAN

Ernan and Phyllis Forbes Dennis were a truly remarkable couple with an exciting and varied life who lived all over Europe after World War I, in which Ernan was severely wounded.* They spent time in Marseilles, where he held an army post. This I believe was a very tough assignment — then they went to Vienna, which was in ruins and rags and much below starvation level. Phyllis's novel *Old Wine* tells the story very clearly, and although it is supposed to be fiction, it gives a very true tale with many real characters woven into the intricate tapestry of the writing. Later throughout the years, they moved into the Austrian Tirol, where Ernan ran a training establishment in languages for young men and Phyllis continued with her writing. She wrote prodigiously and undertook many lecture tours as well. They had a prolonged and difficult courtship before World War I, as Phyllis's life had often been in danger from pulmonary tuberculosis. She witnessed the death of many of her friends in sanatoria in Switzerland. Because of her own illness, her marriage to Ernan had been opposed by his family, and did not take place for a long time. In the end, all turned out well and they spent their lives benefiting many others. When I had the good fortune of being a guest of theirs, they gave frequent soirées, with beautiful classical music. Ernan was an exquisite pianist and was friendly with many gifted musicians. I was always included in the entertainment with my Highland dancing, and had the good fortune to have many outstanding musicians to play for me. Their music was exquisite, but always lacked the dominating first beat as demonstrated by the fiddlers at Blair

* Ernan was the son of one of the Forbeses of Inverernan who married a minister called Dennis.

The author at Brux with 'Stolen Day', September 1952. (*By kind permission of Aberdeen Journals Ltd.*)

Castle to Yehudi Menuhin, with whom I am proud to claim
kinship now that his delightful son has married my youngest
niece.

I was well trained in the beat of Scots and Highland music,
as many long years ago, I played regularly with the Aberdeen
Strathspey and Reel Society, under the inspiring conductorship
of Alec Sim. The glorious thrill of music that coursed in my
'Scots bleed' sent me wild with delight, and of course had a far
more profound effect upon my dancing than ever the special
distillates of the barley bree! I recollect a retired major of the
gallant Cameronians who played a cello which had belonged to
his wife's ancestor, the Scots fiddler and composer, William
Marshall. He at one time was chief butler to Jane, Duchess of
Gordon, who gave salons for the literati of her day in
Edinburgh. Robert Burns read his new poem 'A Winter Night'
on one occasion to such people as the Law Lord, Lord
Monbaddo, Professor Blaikie and many more.

The venerable major was carried away by the soul-filling
beauty of the web of melody that surrounded him. We were
sometimes divided into quartets and competed against each
other. I remember once winning a competition like this,
entirely due to the skill of the other players.

EICHSTÄTT

About the mid 1930s my brother asked if I would accompany
him to Eichstädt in Bavaria, before he set out on a solo flight in
a Puss Moth to Australia. His elder daughter was at the
convent school there, and the younger one we were going to
take out with us. We were going to stay at the guest house of
Saint Walpurga's Nunnery, established I think about the
fourteenth century. It certainly was a wonderful historic
building, in a little town full of churches, seminaries and
colleges, all Roman Catholic. I did not feel very anxious to go,
but as my brother had no other relation to turn to, and nobody
else approved of his renunciation of our Protestant faith, I least

of all, but I felt I owed him some brotherly care. It was to be a very interesting experience. St Walpurga's Nunnery was sacked by Gustavus Adolphus, and the Lady Abbess of that day escaped through a concealed door of a wardrobe and down through a secret stair. This, we were shown during our stay there, as the Bishop of Eichstätt granted permission to the Lady Abbess to take my brother and myself behind what they call the 'Enclosure' which are the premises only inhabited by nuns. When we reached a kind of reception hall, I was requested to do Highland dances, and remember doing Sean Triubhas, accompanied by Willie whistling 'Whistle ower the lave o't'. I don't think such excitement had ever been experienced before by these sweet and kindly women with their hard lives.

We were given a very instructive tour of the bakery the kitchen premises and the garden, saw the bottling of fruit and vegetables, and the care of the dairy, poultry and pigs. All manual labour was performed by the nuns in their most cumbersome garments. I remember that it was at the time when Hilter started his 'Winterhilfe', but these good women fed one hundred people every day, who came to a little window and solicited food. I was full of admiration for their diligence. Besides taking in novices, they had a lot of very old retired ladies-in-waiting from the Bavarian Court who were widowed, and spent their last days in retirement at the convent. They were all most interesting people to converse with. The Lady Abbess herself, was a woman of exceptional knowledge and ability. She belonged to an old Westphalian family and became a nun before World War I, and was housed at a convent in Belgium. It was thought prudent to send her back to Germany, but on no account in nun's clothing, as these people were always suspected of being spies. Accordingly, her civilian clothing was looked out. Some time having elapsed since she had last worn it, she described how, with a Herculean struggle, she had thrust her limbs into the various apertures and eventually emerged as a Michelin-attired civilian! She had a wonderful sense of humour, which was never lacking. I was greatly enthralled by the wonderful oak beams 12–18 inches in width, of which all the floors were made, and of course scrubbed lily-white. The doors were solid oak preserved with linseed, and all hinged with massive and wonderfully designed steel hinges and snecks.

My brother had not informed me of the plan for the following day. He had made arrangements with the Bishop of Eichstätt to receive him officially into the Roman Catholic Faith, and at about 7 am, we foregathered at a private chapel, with very few people present. Theresa Neumann, a truly simple and delightful Bavarian peasant who is well-known to those of her faith as a stigmatist, had agreed to be the Godmother at the said ceremony. After all the rites were performed, we were invited to breakfast at the Bishop's Palace, and I made fast friends with Theresa, as I could speak her dialect. We conversed all the time about agriculture, as she was of farming stock. She could not get over the fact that we produced arable crops in Scotland from spring sowing. Her poor hands and feet were deeply scarred with square marks and she wore mittens and always thick soft slippers. I was disconcerted because she never ate anything which I passed to her, whereas I was guilty of a very hearty appetite.

The Bishop of Eichstätt later became the Roman Catholic Bishop of Berlin, and defied Hitler on many occasions.

While in Eichstätt, I met a very scholarly man called Professor Wutz, who was doing a new translation of the Bible. He was one of the world's greatest speakers of Aramaic. He very kindly wrote out the Lord's Prayer for me in Aramaic, its original language, which I still keep as a rare treasure.

MY FIRST VERY OWN LABRADOR

I had longed to possess my own shooting dog for many a long year, but as everyone was more privileged than I, it was always the kindness of the good keeper and family friend Wattie McBain to lend me one, as I was not allowed to keep it in the house. Eventually, Wattie gave me a beautiful big yellow

The author with 'Bran' outside Craigievar Castle, 1944.

labrador dog of the Braeroy strain, which he had bred and trained himself. This beloved and sagacious animal attached himself to me immediately. He stayed at the kennels, but we always joined company when I had a half day or weekend off. One night, just before I was due to go on holiday to my mother's little house, she rang me up and said she was somewhat alarmed, because there were strange noises at her front door. She had shouted from the upper floor but nobody replied. I was tied on duty at the hospital that night, but suggested that she should ring the police. As it was wartime, she did not want to put the local policeman to any bother, so she went to bed and decided not to worry. In the morning when daylight came, she went down to the front door and there on the mat was my precious dog Bran called after the legend of the old Highland chief, who possessed a dog so brave that he would tackle a monster. The legend goes that his master set him on a monster three times, but it was so terrifying that he always ran away. The third time, he dug in the earth until he disappeared from view and up sprang the river Bran which has been Strathbran ever since. My mother took him into the house where he was waiting for me when I got out of hospital. On another occasion on a very hot summer's day, my dear mother was once again expecting me home for a weekend. As usual, she had been gardening and finally was driven inside to change her clothes. She was standing in her bedroom, having pulled off every stitch, when she became aware there were heavy footsteps ascending the stair. She called out 'Who's there?' — no reply, then 'Wait a minute' but still the steps approached. Pulling her dressing-gown round her, she awaited with some apprehension, and round the door came the handsome copper-coloured Bran.

He became so well mannered and house trained, that he was allowed to stay in the house and an invitation was extended to him by my landlady in town to come in with me and stay in Aberdeen. He would lie at the garden gate with his paws crossed and everyone, especially children walking past, paid court to him. He also went for ploys on his own, and I once passed him on my way to Casualty, going down Carden Place from Mannofield.

Presently, my poor dog was smitten with distemper and pneumonia and was suffering from fearful paroxysms of coughing, very like whooping cough. I would sit up with him at night and treated him as the vet prescribed on M&B tablets. He made a wonderful recovery, but later in life, the M&B tablets had crystallised in the kidneys and impeded the normal passage of urine. Many years after, he would wake me in the middle of the night by putting his paws on my pillow. I realised he was in dire distress and there was no possibility of getting him outside without an accident. I got hold of a Spode chanty pot and stuck it under him and he let go and remained there until the job was completed. It was only occasionally that this happened. He had various houses where he was a welcome visitor and one very dear lady kept scraps for him in her roasting tin. One Monday morning he called upon her, several streets away, and finding the door open he walked in and found the pleasant remains of Sunday's roast, which was much to his taste. I was much upset about this wartime scarcity being devoured, but the dear lady said 'it wasn't Brannie's fault, because he knew she always put his scraps in her roasting dish'.

He was a splendid retriever and water dog, and I enjoyed his tireless company for many years. My best times have always been shared with keepers. There are two keeper neighbours who are always helping me in many ways, and recently during the prolonged storm and gales, they were the people who showed concern that I would get my diabetic medicines from Alford, which touched me greatly.

DROWNING ACCIDENTS IN DON

During the latter part of World War I, my sister went down to swim in the Don, supervised by my mother in a very old fashioned fish-tail tartan skirt and busy knitting a kilt stocking for my father. It was summer holiday time, but the rules about swimming in the Don were strict on account of the dangerous currents. My recollection was that I heard my sister screaming and saw her disappearing beneath the surface of the water. My mother who was close beside me plunged in with all her voluminous garments and swam strongly out towards the sinking body. Unfortunately she had no knowledge of life-saving technique, plus being severely hampered by the tight stays of the day, and other garments in addition to which there was a tiresome thing dragging heavily behind which was the half-wyvan stocking firmly attached to her by the ball of wool in her jacket pocket. She reached my sister who surfaced again, but beat about her with her arms and nearly caused another tradgedy. Fortunately a cousin was also with us and she acted promptly and rescued the drowning girl in the correct fashion, for which she was later decorated with the Silver Life-saving Medal. The foal-at-foot (me) was left roaring and bellowing on the sand bed, at the sight of my dear Mamma disappearing across the river and leaving me behind, for eventually she landed on the opposite shore. It ended without loss of life, but stopped all chance of being allowed to swim in the Don until I became a trusted swimmer as the years passed. At that time, I was about four years old. Unfortunately, there were a number of accidental drownings in the Don in the comparatively quiet waters of Fintray, even in fairly recent times. A young farm worker went in for a 'dook' on a very hot day about lunch time, and in spite of the fact that he was in company with a number of other young lads, he was drowned. Then during the war, one of the recruits in training camp at Fintray was drowned during an exercise with his platoon.

I have rather a rambling but factual tale to tell of the experiences of the head-keeper and myself one Sunday morning. It was one of my Sundays off duty from Casualty, and I had promised Wattie McBain to lie in wait and watch a very illegal operation on the part of fishing tenants on Fintray waters, and be a witness to his observations. They were fishing illegally on Sunday and also with set lines, which was done by setting up forked sticks every ten or twelve yards, baited with maggots. Their method was to shower maggots on the water round about to attract the trout, and then put up these set lines.

Of course, if anyone were watching, they fiddled about, but did not carry out the operation. We lay down on our bellies on the river embankment which was constructed to prevent flooding in times of spate. Things were about to develop when a few loons came along the river and we had to wait until they had moved on. The people we were watching were on the opposite bank and things were settling down nicely once more when an old tramp came along, removed all his clothes and proceeded to sit in the shallow water and have his annual bath. This was a very lengthy affair, so once again the fishing ploy was frustrated. Eventually, this also came to an end, and at last the coast was clear. The maggoting method was put into action and I noted all that I had been asked to witness, and then all of a sudden a policeman appeared walking down the Inverurie/ Aberdeen railway line, and Wattie announced, 'There's been a droonin'.' 'Oh, maybe somethin' else Wattie.' 'Oh na, I'm sure it's a droonin'.' Sure enough it was. We felt that we must make our presence known, and be of any assistance to the constable, which of course, blew our cover, but by this time we had our evidence. The corpse was duly discovered at Bieldestone, which was some distance down the water.

I am glad to say that both my parents were plain speaking and unpretentious folk. My mother was constantly bringing me up on the words 'be humble' and the auld man was much taken up with simple ploys, especially if it meant making an escape from grandiose visitors. At that time, he usually went down to what was commonly known as the muck-burnie, which was a ditch which ran from a swamp along the bottom of the four acre garden and thence at the lower part of the terrace below Fintray House, down to the River Don. As it had very little fall and therefore practically no flow, it needed constant clearing and raking with what was known as a creeper, which was a curved graip. This was always the ideal ploy and escape from boring visitors. He also delighted in incognito chats with workmen who might have been employed on some special job. One day, there were two nice chaps putting in a service lift which was hauled up by a rope from the kitchen premises to the pantry passage behind the dining room, to save many tiring journeys to the domestic staff. The gun-room was just alongside and my father in an old knickerbocker suit was working on some piece of sporting equipment. One chap said 'Foo lang hiv ye been here keeper?' The reply was, 'O a gey lang file, but I'm nae gaun tae bide'. 'O fit wye?' 'I canna thole the laird' was the prompt reply. The arrival of an employee to seek the laird's advice about some matter brought this promising conversation to an untimely end.

MARRIED IN 1952

Having joined the Auld Kirk at Kildrummy, my wife and I were married by the minister, the Revd Peter MacEwen, in October 1952. We had a quiet wedding with only a chosen few real friends and relations, followed by a very merry ceilidh at Brux, at which most of the guests contributed their musical share in the entertainment. Members of my concert party were much appreciated and sang and played beautifully. Mrs Cowe never had a moment's leisure from the keyboard. Presently we had a cold turkey and champagne supper party, followed by cognac and liqueurs. It was an evening of much happiness and delight. Twenty-five years later, we celebrated our Silver Wedding with a dinner and ceilidh at Kildrummy Castle Hotel, though sad to relate that some of our very dear friends had passed on. Our good minister and his wife came up specially for the occasion.

BECOMING AN ELDER

Although declining when first asked, I consented later and was most honoured and very happy when the minister requested me to be one of his Elders. I have enjoyed so much worshipping in the plain but beautiful simplicity of Kildrummy Kirk and having my own district of folk to look after. It was in a way like

Bride and groom, 10 October 1952. (*All photographs of wedding and presentation are by courtesy of Mr Alex Morrison, Lumphanan.*)

Wedding Ceilidh at Brux 10 October 1952; left to right David Forbes, tenor, best man; James Cowe, baritone; the Bride; Mrs Cowe, pianist.

having people to be responsible for like patients in the practice, but of course, on so much smaller a scale. In my practice, I worked in no fewer than nine nursing districts, which meant covering a large area. My very special nurse was always our own dear Mrs Royan in Alford. What joy it brings to worship the Lord and enjoy Him for ever.

WEDDING PRESENTATION

About a month after we were married, we received a wonderful wedding presentation from my dear patients. The folk from the glens moved down to Alford in a solid body to watch the late Mr MacDonald, the slater, present us with a beautiful Regency desk, a very fine dirk and some special cases and luggage for my wife. Thereafter, we entertained them to tea and a concert. There was a special new Scottish country dance composed complete with music by Miss Alice McLennan and called 'The Doctor's Waddin'. Together with a number of my dancing friends who took part in this, I joined in the performance. There are two photographs to show the number of my patients present at this enthusiastic celebration. No wonder I felt such a sadness at having to give up my practice. I have never really got over the disappointment. My one solace was that Dr Manson was able to come back and I knew that he would cherish and look after all my dear folk, as he was such a reliable and trustworthy colleague, and together with his splendid wife, would see that nothing and no one was neglected. He deserves true appreciation. I was sad beyond belief at having to give up my practice, but my lawyer explained in very frank terms that my grieve had put me in such a serious financial position that I would have to produce cash immediately to cope with the situation, and the best way was to claim my dues on the practice from the Health Service. My only comfort was that my very trusted colleague, Dr Manson, was willing to be appointed, and I knew he would always do his best to look after my dear folk.

Alford patients in Village Hall, Alford, 14 November 1952. (*By kind permission of Aberdeen Journals Ltd.*)

Wedding presentation to author and his wife by Mrs Peter MacEwan and Mr William McDonald on behalf of the patients.

Wedding gifts presented by Mr W. McDonald.

ALCOHOL

Our parental upbringing regarding alcohol was organised with much wisdom. During years of adolescence, if claret was served at dinner, we were encouraged to take with caution, smacking our lips to get the true taste, and of course, looking at the light through the glass to see that the wine was clear, and using the nose with discretion to appreciate the bouquet. Naturally, all these finer points took time to learn and appreciate and the amount of wine allowed, would probably be about two tablespoonsful. No spirits were ever allowed. Sherry and madeira were produced on festive occasions, also occasionally liqueurs. I must admit I was longing to taste whisky, but would never have dreamt of breaking the family law, as it would have appeared like breaking faith in view of the gentlemanly privileges allowed.

One fine summer evening, I went down for a swim in the Don, but on arriving at the Silver Strand, I found the poor old Clydesdale mare who worked on the Home Farm, stuck deep in the mud at the bottom end of the sand bank. She suffered from what is known as a 'shot of grease' in a hind leg, which is an affliction of the lymphatic system accompanied by much swelling. The poor old beast had waded into the river to drink and no doubt to cool her legs, but she went into this area where the mud was very tenacious, and the more she had struggled, the deeper she sank, till the water was over her back and she was shivering with cold and exhaustion. I waded in beside her with easy freedom, having only my bathing suit. I felt all round the tops of her legs, but found that no movement was possible. I ran back the half mile to the house and raised the alram for farm personnel and neighbours to come with all speed and bring ropes. About twenty-five men appeared in remarkably quick time. I then wriggled in beside Auld Kate and bored with my hands to get the ropes pushed through round each leg. After struggling for about two hours, we got her pulled out. As each leg became freed, she walloped and slashed my bare shins. By this time, I was feeling very chilled in spite of the warm evening, so a hot bath was just the thing, but imagine my delight when my mother said a good dram of whisky would be the best thing for me to take!

Strangely, many years later, when enjoying a weekend off from University, I was swimming further down the Don, when a Clydesdale appeared stranded in the same manner, but on the othe side of the river. Swimming across and running over two fields, I hailed the farm staff at Pitmedden, who came forthwith from their haymaking and rescued the poor beast.

THE TALE OF THE WHITE DOVE

My recollection of Sundays, with the exception of the delights of Mr Barr's sermon for the children, and the journeying to and from Kinellar Kirk, was that Sunday afternoon was always given over to walking from Fintray to put flowers on my sister's grave, at the old Kirkyard of St Meddans which was once the parish church, both in pre-Reformation days and then again after 1560 when a Scottish Act of Parliament decreed the Scottish Reformation. The Auld Kirk became the Forbes Family Mausoleum for Fintray, and the first Laird to be buried there was Sir Arthur Forbes 4th Bart, with the charming inscription on his tombstone, 'Worthy of a longer life had it so pleased Heaven.' Being only about five years old, I became very bored by the routine walk and circumspection, so I went on small ploys round the kirkyard. On one of these I discovered a broken 'globie' with a beautiful white dove lying beside it — poor thing, it must be cold and lonely, so I put it in my jacket pocket and carried it home. Later that night, my mother found me fast asleep in my bed, holding the bonnie doo close to my face. Next morning, she asked, 'Where did you get the white dove?' When I told her, she appeared to be very angry, and ordered me to take it back the moment lessons were finished, but I was allowed to ride, which was a pleasure never permitted on a Sunday.

TWO OLD TIME STORIES

The Aberdeen trams were widely known for the cheapness of their fares, and in my University days, I travelled many miles for 1d. Likewise for no doubt a cheaper rate, my father also made frequent use of them when he served at the old King Street Barracks. One day he found himself sitting beside a wee loon to whom he said, 'Faur are ye guan laddie?' The animated reply was, 'There's been a murder at Widside, an' I'm guan doon tae see the bleed!' No doubt a splendid bawbee's worth.

Our Pekingese with tame Roe deer fawn.

Another recollection of my father, was about a time he was travelling in Germany with some other young people and one evening they had a ceilidh at which he played his pipes well into the late hours of the night. He was arrested by the police and kept under detention until daylight for causing a disturbance during the hours of rest in the city of Darmstadt. My wife and I, while on a caravan holiday complete with a vizsla and a spaniel, were having a pleasant picnic by a magnificent Ross-shire waterfall when a troup of bright and laughing young people came up and asked most politely if they could take my photograph as I was wearing the kilt. They asked if I could play Duddelsack, but I explained I did not have them with me. I told them the story about my father, which convulsed them with laughter and they promised to regale their friends at home in Stuttgart with the tale.

GARDEN PARTIES AND BORES

Before the war, it was considered the done thing for all big houses to give at least one large party in the year, to which all neighbours from nearby counties were invited. It was a bore, and a boon at the same time, as the large numbers entertained each other and were all dealt with at one fell swoop. My mother was very dutiful in fulfilling her social obligations, and of course, if I happened to be at home at the time, I could not fail her by not helping with the guests. 'Garden Parties' were definitely the most boring of all entertainments. The chief bores always arrived on the dot or possibly even a little earlier. I devised a plan which I expounded to my dear mother with some success — put the time on the invitation quarter of an hour later for the moderate bores, and half an hour later for the super bores. This was most successful, and ensured having about one hundred guests already established before the dreaded ones arrived. Later on I persuaded her to make her entertainment a sherry party, which encouraged people to greater volubility after the consumption of some alcohol. The chatter increased one-hundred-fold and there was very little effort on our part, except to ply them well with eats and drinks, which were done in a superb manner, as my mother excelled at catering and had an excellent cuisine.

Of course, there were many people whose company was much enjoyed and more intimate meals were devised for them. One such occasion was code-named 'Baronial Sanitation throughout the Ages', when my sister and I collected together all the strange commodes and conveniences of a bygone age, including some with cute little steps to climb up to some of the fourposters about five feet off the ground. The top step lifted to reveal a chanty-pot inside! The special friends were invited to dinner and thereafter my mother said she wanted them to see some interesting antiques. There were some beautiful mahogany bidets with the insides removed which had been fitted with music of Liszt and Chopin Waltzes, and used as piano stools. Commodes came in various forms, some like regal thrones with steps for the feet, and some with formidable handle bars at the sides for the more serious gripping moments. The exhibition was a great success in entertainment.

One summer evening, I suggested that we should serenade a charming couple, a French Baron and his wife. So we dressed up like tinkies and made a cautious approach to their house I played the piano accordian and my mother sang. She was well wrapped round with a plaidie. Eventually, the Baron appeared, whereupon my normally very cultured Mamma lurched sideways and pretended she had been regaling herself with spirits, and asked him for a contribution. He called upstairs to his wife to throw down sixpence, and she replied in an audible whisper, '3d is plenty.' We could not contain our laughter any more and burst into peals of hilarity! I don't think our foreign friends could believe their eyes or their ears.

FISHING WITH SUCCESS

My apologies to the reader who may not be at all interested in angling, but on various occasions there have been entertaining experiences. One of these was in March 1959, long before we expect to have salmon high up the Don. I realised that the water was far too cold for the fly and fixed myself up with a very Heath-Robinson spinning outfit. There was so much work to do that it was always about 6 pm before a start could be made. I hooked a fish about 9 lb and landed it, followed by a second and was well aware of the likelihood of the line breaking. Then, still at the same pool, I hooked a third, and he was just beginning to tire nicely and come in close to the bank, when I realised he was floating down the water quite unattached. For once I decided on drastic action, pulled out my gaff and ran down the bank alondside. Leaning over the edge, I made a quick and firm upwards cleek, and had him on the bank. I had always thought this was impossible and had even told a famous author so. I offer sincere apologies for mis-informing her, and causing her to change the story she was writing!

I had another entertaining experience with three salmon one morning about eight o'clock. I wasn't catching anything on the fly, but I was informed by some of my fishing tenants that the people who were fishing opposite my beat were catching a lot of salmon on spinning minnows. Accordingly I started down the pool, spinning. With the first cast I hooked a fish, ran it and tailed it. I cast again, was taken at the second cast and again tailed it, but I did not notice that the point of my little rod was bending so acutely that it snapped. Well, being determined not to give up on that account, I removed the cast and bait, pulled off the broken tip and connected up the cast and bait again. This left me with a jagged point sticking out, and line emerging from the second ferrule, not so easy for casting, but once again at the second cast, another fish was on. I pulled his head up the steep bank and grabbed his tail. In the meantime the bait fell out of his mouth, and with a quick clunk on the back of the head, he was added to the bag. Home in an hour from starting, there were three fish, two of 8 lb and on 8¼ lb, to show for my morning venture. That little rod cost me £3 in 1959, and apart from the new point, did not disintegrate until the end of 1982. How I miss my old rod! and how often alas does one draw a blank.

OTTERS

Having employed single assistants in my practice over a period of years, I had the opportunity of a married assistant with more of a possibility of his settling down for some years, so I moved up to Brux and set Rosemount House vacant for his family to occupy. Shortly afterwards, I got married and we set up our home at Brux. My wife found the peace and solitude a bit lonely for a start after the bustle of reception and looking after the housekeeping for me and my doctors, but eventually, it became very much home. On my evenings off, there was a wonderful opportunity for instructing her in fishing. One evening just at dusk, she was casting a bonny line, when suddenly a head appeared out of the water just at her rod tip, whiskers bristled, and it blew! She gave one blood-curdling scream and it vanished. I was talking to an old rabbit trapper in the background and we both said, 'Wheest', but alas too late, as the beautiful but shy otter vanished with a powerful swish of his tail, leaving a large wake. 'Ye'll never get an opportunity to see the like of that again.' We have forbidden the killing of otters at Brux, and the eel population is well under control. One met by an accidental death many years ago and I had him made into a beautiful sporran. There are some about, but unfortunately not nearly so many as there used to be. Sadly, some of them are run over while crossing the road.

MY GOAL ACHIEVED AT LAST

In 1939, I was accepted as a medical student at Aberdeen University. What a wonderful moment to have reached, after the crushing rejection by my father. I had plodded on, making finances for my fees and digs, and at last could hardly believe that the wonderful moment had actually arrived. I felt very shy of the other students, who were almost all about ten years younger, and much better versed in scientific subjects, such as chemistry and physics, and even maths of which my knowledge was most elementary, as I had had more of a literary and arts education, in Europe. They were such a likeable lot of chaps and girls and so willing to assist me in my ignorance. Of course, they were full of beans and fun, sometimes a bit tiring for someone who had had to settle down to earn his living in a rather precarious manner ten years earlier. Time soon ironed out the differences. We were very much a body full of 'esprit de corps', and resented bossy and unnecessary rules and regulations levelled at us. I recollect that we had a short cut from the Maternity Hospital down to the hostel which apparently was disapproved. A fence about 5 feet high with six strands of barbed wire was erected. Within a couple of nights, a little prank was played which appeased our natural resentment.

Our class (1939–44) covered the war years, and with fire-watching, auxiliary ambulance service, auxiliary mortuary service and many other extra duties, including the cutting out of two summer vacations to cram in extra terms, was very hard work. Indeed, I am sure it accounted for the loss of the valuable life of one of our most popular and brilliant students. In October 1944, after having met almost every day for five years, we were capped and dispersed to our different jobs. I applied for the post of Junior Casualty Officer, and to my great joy I got it. I never valued anything more than the enormous amount of work and responsibility the post brought me. It was my very good fortune to have Sister Stopani as the Sister in charge of Casualty. Her vast knowledge from the days when

she was Theatre Sister to the late Sir Henry Gray operating in
the front line in World War I, was tremendous. She taught me
so many of his skills with local anaesthetics, keeping head
wounds bare whenever possible and many other precious
secrets. My assistants and part-time assistants from the Medical
and VD departments, were all splendid doctors, mostly from
my class and we worked very happily together.

Later on, I had the good fortune to become Senior Casualty
Officer. Many were the experiences we had in that wonderful
place. There were all the usual street accidents great and
small, frequent attempted suicides, many stopped fortunately
just in time. I remember after bringing round one fairly far
gone case following a lot of work, she looked up and said, 'I
wish I wis deid.' On reflection, I realised how desperately
disappointing it must have been to meet with failure, after
planning everything in great detail. In those days, coal gas
poisoning from the cooker was by far the most popular means.
My first day in Casualty was saddened by the death of a third-
year medical student, whom we worked with for some considerable time, with no response. Fortunately I benefited from the
presence of the previous Senior Casualty Officer, who was still
in charge for some days.

There was a regular attendance of epileptics who fell down
in the street and were always brought in to us by the police
ambulance. The drivers of these ambulances were great friends
of the Casualty doctors, and we were always ready to help each
other out. One day I recollect in particular. A police
ambulance arrived with a man badly scalded about the legs.
His wife came with him, but there was no particular story
about how this had occurred. The patient was laid on the
couch in what we called 'the police room'. I examined him
immediately and ordered the dressings to be prepared and
hurried to get him a pain-killing injection. When I returned a
moment later, the man had vanished! I suddenly became
aware of stentorian breathing, but still there was no one to be
seen. There was no one in front of the couch and only the space
of a very few inches between the couch and the wall at the
back. Recognising a well-known sound, his wife rushed

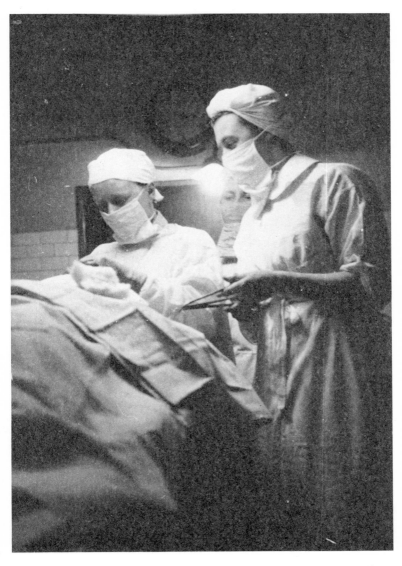

Author operating in Casualty Theatre at Woolmanhill with Sister
Isobel McDonald, 1944.

through the Casualty Department from the waiting hall, crying, 'Willie Drystie! Drystie Willie!' I realised immediately the whole of the drama. The poor man had had a fit and pulled a pot of boiling water over his legs at home — he was brought to hospital without any explanation. He landed in an amazing tangle with his head and torso through about half a dozen old motor tyres which were stored beneath the couch for making walking pieces on plasters for patients with leg fractures. Fortunately the extra fit had quelled the pain in the meantime and allowed us to disentangle him from his awkward bedfellows!

One simple little tale comes to mind about a man who arrived one day with a complaint of frequency. When it was enquired, 'What is your job?', he replied, 'A lavatory attendant'! Another time, a fairly aged wifie arrived with a dreadful black eye. I said, 'Tell me what happened' A lady hit ma', was her prompt reply!

MY TWENTY-FIRST BIRTHDAY SHOOT

As a youngster, my great sporting ambition was to be a game shot. In early days, I bought an air gun, and practised target shooting. After my seventeenth birthday, I approached my father with caution about getting a shotgun. The usual answer was 'Hm we'll see'. Finally he bought the cheapest second-hand sixteen bore, and I was sent out with the keeper to kill rabbits. After firing twenty-six shots and killing twenty-three rabbits, no adverse comment was made, and shortly permission was given to shoot game, which proved no difficulty. It gradually produced problems, however, as my father was inclined to be jealous and when other guns praised my shooting, he could be very annoyed. On the other hand, if my day had been less successful, scolding inevitably followed, so which ever way things went, I was in the dog house.

My enthuasiasm was boundless and the old keeper used to make remarks like 'If ye gied doon a lum ye'd get sheetin' (If

you went down a chimney, you would get shooting) or 'Ye'd
sheet yer mither if she could flee' (You would shoot your
mother is she could fly). Anyway, it was all tremendously
enjoyable. It was after I started shooting, that my urge to own
a dog became ever greater. I am sure that those people who
don't own and work their own dog, miss the greatest enjoyment
of all, the team work of achieving the heights together, with
the understanding and companionship of a real friend, who is
dedicated to doing his or her best for you at all times. Real
understanding is so important. No hitting or scolding is
necessary if your entente is really complete. Patience and time
must be given, but the reward is so great. I feel that the
sportsman who could own a dog, and doesn't, is really a
creature to be much pitied. On the other hand, perhaps it is
fortunate for the dog not to have such a master. All creatures
thrive on love. Chaucer's Lady Prioress had a brooch whereon
was writ, 'Amor Vincit Omnia' and 'two little doggies had she,
and sic a tenderie hertie that she weepit if man smoot them
with a yairdie smertie.' I belive all animals can be taught to
reciprocate friendship and trust human kind in a few days if
treated in a sensible and understanding way. Nowadays, since
I have given up farming on a large scale and do not have a
permanent staff, my policy is to buy yearling cattle in the
spring and in three days' time, have them eating out of my
hand and even out of my mouth, When I want to move them, I
just call and they follow my little four wheel drive vehicle and
we move from one pasture to another.

My father was a very right-minded sportsman, and very dis-
approving of greedy shooting of birds definitely heading for
other guns. He also deplored the use of shot below No.
7 – 'Ruins the birds,' he always said, and how I agree with him.
At my request, my wife has made a study of the culinary results
of the flesh of grouse, pheasants and partridges, which are
dessicated and dried up as a result of too close shooting and the
use of large pellets. He was also a stickler for the usual habitat
of birds. For instance, on the march between Fintray and
Straloch, where our cousins lived, when birds flew uphill
towards the Straloch coverts, he would roar down the line,

'Don't shoot, they belong to Straloch.' This is sadly not the norm at the present time of much ill-mannered behaviour in the shooting field.

Straloch and Barra bring back memories of many happy days shooting with my late cousin Quentin Irvine and his charming and delightful wife with her wonderful sense of humour. As a young shot, they made me feel a fully fledged sportsman. This kindly treatment has been enjoyed up to the present time with the good laird and his son.

Although my father was given of a fiery and ill temper, he had a very kindly outlook for the old and infirm. He was a very fine fisherman. One day the Bishop of Aberdeen was fishing as a guest on Fintray and was accompanied by his wife and an old lady. The old lady suddenly stepped on the point of his 17-foot salmon rod, shattering it to splinters. I thought the result would be awful, but all he said was, 'Puir aul bitch, she mann hae been awfa' blin'!' A story comes to mind at this moment, about the same Bishop, who came out for a day ferreting rabbits. This would have been over fifty years ago. The old keeper in attendance said the Bishop fired shot after shot, with no satisfactory result. The Reverend gentleman observed, 'I cannot understand it. I was at Esslemont last week and shot forty rabbits with forty-two shots.' The auld keeper, pulling his ragged whiskers, said, 'But ye ken, even a Bishop files tells a bit lee.'

The officers from Castlehill Barracks were frequently entertained to my father's shoots, and punctuality was included in the list of shooting manners. One of these chaps reminded me recently of a very unsatisfactory subaltern who arrived late. My father regarded him severely and said, 'You are four minutes late, you can go back to barracks now.'

Before my twenty-first birthday, my mother asked me what sort of party I would like for my celebration. I said 'A shoot, please.' 1933 was a wonderful year weather-wise, and came in the middle of several matchless years of good nesting and hatching seasons. I chose my guns because of their ability to walk and shoot — they were my kinsman, the late Sir John Forbes of Newe, Bart. The late Dandie Wallace of Candacraig and Nigel Ferguson of Pitfour, with whom I have lost touch. We had a glorious day, sporting and weather wise, ending up with seventy-five brace of partridges, an all-time record for Craigievar, from the time bags were recorded in 1861 down to the present time. I still have the gifts which I received from these old friends, including Lady Forbes of Newe who was engaged to Sir John, and married him shortly afterwards. It was really a day of evergreen memories.

My appreciation of shooting is not one of big days and large bags, but rather of a few real sporting shots, like falling down a rocky hillside and shooting a blackcock while my feet found themselves in the air and I was 'coupit' on my back!, shooting a right and left of snipe while being firmly hooked up by my kilt in a barbed wire fence, or shooting a tremendously high pheasant. Long and exhilarating tramps in rough ground were always my delight. Of course, the occasional big grouse drive could be very exciting, but I never appreciated the point of view of lazy young men who wanted to sit all day and have birds driven over them. In the past few years, I began to realise that there were a number of people who considered themselves very important, and were such an obnoxious bore, that they spoiled the whole day out for many a jolly sportsman. In the long run, I decided to decline to be a guest on occasions when such people were likely to be there. I had an old friend, a retired indigo planter, who had a wealth of experience both here and in India, in spite of being very seriously hampered by a badly deformed leg, the result of polio at the age of six. This did not stop him from walking on the hill or through parks of 'neeps'. He always had a walking stick, and when birds got up, the stick would appear to fly with the covey, followed by the immediate fall of a right and left of birds. He taught me that when walking into a covey, you could easily shoot two birds and shove just one more cartridge into the breach and have time to shoot a third bird, whereas if you attempted to reload two cartridges, everything would be out of shot. I never heard him complain of his severe disability. This old friend's wife was a girlhood acquaintance of my aunt, and at one time, the two households used to live close beside each other. The old sportsman used to employ a 'loon' who was rather mentally impaired, but he did some gardening and odd jobs, including carrying things between the households. My old friend always took the sporting periodical *The Field* which he lent to my aunt to read. One day the 'feel loon' arrived at her door and said, 'He's needin' *The Park* back'!

COUNTRY PRACTICE

One morning, a call came for a boy with a sore throat, I found my way to an old house at the top of a long brae and was welcomed by a pleasant smiling-faced mother who said, 'It's Alickie, doctor, he was an awfu' bad birth, an' he's never come tae richt.' She obviously regarded him as delicate and was worried about this sore throat. I reassured her and got him on to the everlasting standby of M&B tablets. During the time I was examining him, there were some very rough blows on the kitchen door. The lad was reclining on a couch, well covered with a rug. The mother looked apprehensive and smothered several exclamations into her hankie. I thought there must be another child who had been excluded and was annoyed about it, and making its presence heard. All of a sudden, there was the sound of wood being shattered, and a beautiful curled horn emerged through one of the panels. The housewife exclaimed, 'It's the tame lambie, doctor.' I asked her where she would like it to be shut in, pushed back the magnificent horn, applied my knee to its tail end and steered it by its handle-bars into the shed she indicated. It certainly had been the 'tame lambie' once upon a time, but long since had become a handsome adult. I became fast friends with these delightful people, and in due course spend an evening at a home confinement there, which took place in the best room, with a large bed and a piano. The patient never made a sound of complaint, but rolled about and turned somersaults all the time. It struck me as incongrous, that here in the midst of new life, we were surrounded by endless photographs of poor Jocks

Mrs Grant, Centenarian of Alford Practice.

Left to right Mrs Royan, District Nurse, Alford; Mrs Grant, The Pond, Keig; the author — on the celebration of Mrs Grant's Centenary, June 1952. (*By kind permission of Aberdeen Journals Ltd.*)

who had been killed in World War I, or else those sad wooden
crosses erected in the British War Cemeteries. All sadness was
swept away by the miracle of birth and the lusty yells of the
new-born babe. It was a wonderful evening for this event to
take place, as I had spent that very morning assisting a famous
surgeon, in an operation on the husband of our wonderful
district nurse, and no doubt it was the perfect diversion for her
worried heart, when the lusty yell announced the entry of a
hearty new member of our patient's family.

MEDICAL OFFICER TO THE GERMAN PRISONERS OF WAR

There were around thirty German prisoners of war in Alford
about 1946 and whenever they required any medical attention,
they came to my surgery. They were very polite and co-
operative and delighted to find a doctor who could speak to
them in their own langauge, so that symptoms could be
explained direct from patient to physician. The British MO in
charge of the area, hearing of this, appointed me to take
charge of the Prisoners of War Camp at Monymusk, where 800
men were housed. They too were all Germans, but hitherto
repatriation boards were made up of one German MO, one
British MO, and an interpreter. It became quite a bonanza for
me, as I was able to cope with all three offices and was
remunerated accordingly. They were very satisfactory to deal
with and carried out orders in an exemplary manner. I was
never waited upon in such a kindly and efficient manner, one
with a trolley and equipment, one with a mobile washstand,
one with towels and a very able orderly to write down exact
details. They were in very poor shape, having come from a
camp in Belgium where food supplies had been short. One
man 6 feet 7 inches tall weighed less than six stones. It so
happened that I had been very thin following flu and
bronchitis after a hard winter's work and had bought some
Keppler's malt and cod liver oil to buck myself up. I felt that

this poor man was in far greater need, and took the jar down to Monymusk. It certainly did us both a lot of good. I was quite sorry when my prisoners were moved from the Deer Park Camp. Some of the prisoners found jobs on farms and stayed in the district. There were also a few Italians scattered around the area. One came to my surgery one day and said his boss was very ill—'He thinks he gyan tae dee!' I called and found that the illness was basically man-made from the over celebration with the barley bree. Controlling the heart rate soon made him feel well again.

AN UNEXPECTED CONFINEMENT

Another occasion in the hinterland of Cushnie, I was attending a patient with a heart attack late one evening, when just before leaving the farmhouse where this occurred, a tall figure appeared on the doorstep and asked for the doctor to go up to his very remote croft. His wife had told him, 'There's a wommun arrived here the day, an' I'm sure she's gaun tae hae a bairn the nicht.' Fortunately it was very frosty, which froze the fields and track so hard, that it was possible to motor right up to the place. There it proved only too true about the prophecy of the confinement. The patient was duly put to bed in the one and only spare bed in an otherwise empty room, with the exception of a chest of drawers. Charging off home to collect the district nurse and the maternity gear and returning with all speed, the crofter's wife appeared in the moonlight waving a towel and shouting, 'It's here! It's here!' Immediate action stations for the nurse and myself. We were given the only lamp in the house and various bits of childrens' garments to clothe the infant. Then of course, there was no cot so one of the drawers was pulled out of the chest of drawers to lay the baby in. The kindly crofter's wife then said, 'Ye maun a' hae a cup o' tay.' We were all taken into the kitchen with the one and only lamp, leaving the patient to the gentle glow of the firelight. 'Michty me,' exclaimed the housewife, 'I've nae milk, for there's been nae time tae milk the coo.' In the twinkling of an eye, she vanished with the lamp to the byre and left the company at the kitchen fire. In a few minutes, she was back again with some milk in a pail and the ubiquitous lamp! She poured milk into a bowl in the middle of the table, filled the cups with tea and put down an extra cup and said, 'Fa tee an' help yersels.' Making sure that mother and child were all right, we set off for home. Next morning, after surgery, I returned to see how my maternity case was doing. The crofter's wife was scolding because the patient refused to feed or have anything to do with her baby. She told me in forceful tones, how she had handled the situation. 'I said, this is your bairn and ye're guan to feed it. I took the whisky bottle an' rubbit her breists wi' spirit, syne rubbin the bairns moo an' pit it tae — it took a guid haud, an' sookit fine. I bade wi' her tae mak' siccar that she did the job richt!' Thanks to her diligence and her kindly spirit, that baby survived. Fortunately, I was able to set this good women on the road to health, when she had a severe attack of cholecystitis (gall-stones). She had come from the Howe of the Mearns, where she had had several attacks, but the doctors said that at twenty-two she was far too young to have such an affliction. I bundled her into a surgical ward, where she was operated on without delay. To her great delight, she was given a jar with all the gall-stones in it, and she announced with much pride, 'Ye ken there wis abeen a hundard.'

THE CASUALTY DEPARTMENT

The variety of characters and accidents were limitless. The first time I was told that there was a man knocked out by a fish basket, I laughed, little realising that these receptacles held two hundredweight and more of fish, and that anyone unlucky enough to have one lowered carelessly on to his head, was likely to be laid out. The unpleasant accidents that happened to the poor fishermen were legion and their gratitude for surgical attention was touching. How often these old salts pulled a newspaper parcel out of their jacket saying, 'I thocht ye wad like a haddie, Doctor', and indeed, how welcome it was. Their hands were grooved with hacks and sores caused by the salt water. The fishworkers, mostly female, were regular attenders with what they called 'fish pizenin'' which was officially known as the Erysipeloid of Rosenbach. In those days, the only cure was with a black and very unpleasant-smelling dressing called Ichthyol. They arrived in brigades every day.

Then there were the farm workers whose jobs were much more familiar to me. Frequently I had to amputate finger tips after the ends had been caught in a bone davy (manure distributor). Much worse occurred when balers and harvesters were involved, but these were not in wide circulation until a good few years later. I have special reason to remember a stockman with a dislocated shoulder, who had been charged and knocked down by an Aberdeen-Angus bull, and sent in by his doctor for X-ray and treatment. He came from the Alford region and was later to be one of my patients in that practice. I attended him at Casualty, and later on in his own home. One evening at surgery in Alford, he visited me and said he was leaving the district and had come to thank me for all I had done for him. The delightful end to the story was that his name was Turnbull!

One met hundreds of people in a week, and because of the special identification of accidents and diseases, it seemed to be easy to remember them all as individuals. I recollect one man with a small fracture, but noted that he also suffered from a skin disease known as psoriasis. One day many months later, I met him walking down the street, and he called, 'Hullo Doctor.' I must have looked a little blank. 'D'ye nae min' on me wi' my sore-eyes?' I found myself gazing into the eyes for a full sixty seconds before collecting my brains and tumbling to his question.

One day, with screams of pain, a poor woman came tearing in with a towel swathed round her shoulders—she had been scalded with boiling water. I attended to her at once, and she came daily for dressings and over a period of time, I heard the whole sordid story. She lived in a tenement where the wash house was shared by two other families. It was allotted to A on Monday, B on Tuesday and C on Wednesday, and the last three days of the week in the same rotation. My patient's day was Wednesday, but she noticed that the morning was well advanced on Tuesday and the usual occupant had not taken possession, so she thought she would get on with her washing. The other tenant was furious, and made a plan to place a bucket of boilding water on the top of the door on the next day Mrs C would be washing. Her scheme worked with disastrous precision, but the real hurt was that her neighbour accused her of being a prostitute, and she had received a very offensive letter. She said she could not write, and asked if I would write a letter for her. I agreed, if she would come to see me in Casualty on Sunday, as it was the only day I might have a minute to spare.

We had the usual silly jokers, like the chaps who went into a nearby bar and one said, 'I bet ye a roun' o' drinks ye couldna pit this gless up your backside.' 'I bet ye I could', and he did but, alas, it could not be brought down again. After much struggling at Casualty, we had to give up, and he was admitted to hospital for quite a major operation. Speaking of drinks, reminds me of a very pleasant damsel who owned a nearby pub. She comforted herself with a 'wee tootie' fairly frequently, with the unfortunate result that she sometimes missed her footing, and when she fell she always put out her hand and dislocated her thumb. This meant a hasty trip round to me, when I put it back in right shape. She told me that if I needed some whisky or beer at any time, she would be happy to provide it. As this was one of the scarce commodities of war time, I kept it in mind. The general team which ran Out-patients every day, decided that before their time was up, they would celebrate by having a dinner one evening after the Department was closed. It was summer time and no lights were required. The four doctors all volunteered to supply some necessary items, and mine was from my patient with the dislocated thumb. Nurses from farming families provided fabulous chickens, and the porter kept us all right. It was an outstanding and happy success.

THE RESULT OF THE WARMTH OF SPIRIT

An entertaining story of Casualty days comes to mind, when I recollect an evening among friends, with music and drams, when some of our senior colleagues were present. One famous surgeon came as a guest, driven to the party by a well-known physician. When it was time to go home, the physician was not in driving order, so it was agreed that I would drive his car with himself and his friend as passengers. One of the ladies at the party volunteered to accompany me. On the way down Queen's Road, the surgeon, groping about, got hold of her hand. Very cunningly she slipped his hand into that of the physician, and quite happily they held hands all the way down Albyn Place.

CONFINEMENTS IN A BLIZZARD

My ultimate ambition in the field of medicine, was to become a surgeon, but of course, having worked so many years before being able to begin my studies, this posed a further delay in the fulfilment of this goal. I certainly had a very varied and interesting opportunity of much surgical work in Casualty. Apart from dealing with accidents, for three afternoons each week, I did out-patient operations for each of the main surgical wards, which was most instructive. Good fortune came my way in offers to become house-surgeon to John Gerrie or Sandy Mitchell, but I declined their kind invitations because I felt so keen on Casualty. My very old shooting and fishing friend, Gordon Bruce, advised me that it was a long haul in those days to be able to make your way in private surgery, and was very uncertain about what the coming of the Health Service would hold in store for us, so on his advice, I had a go at acquiring the Alford practice. This proved a success, both for me to be 'amang my ain fowk', and I think I may say for them to have somebody who knew their ways, and could speak their language. Dr Knox, the medical superintendant, tried to dissuade me from leaving Woolmanhill, but of course, much as I enjoyed my work there, the chance of Alford might be gone for ever. On 1st November 1945, I started in Alford as a GP. The work was very different from the rush and large numbers of patients at Casualty, but the country folk, and the hame-ower ways were very heart-warming. The battle with the elements in winter was a particularly active one, although my first year was comparatively easy. Nineteen forty-seven showed the teeth of storm and it started snowing about Burns Nicht, never stopping till after 20 March. I vowed that I would never fail to try to get through to any call and kept my vow. I had an old Dodge car like a battleship, and when she had gone as far as she could, my motivation was on skis or snow-shoes, or a borrowed Clydesdale, or whiles in great luxury being driven in some kind fairmer's muck-sledge with the bottom comfortably filled with straw. This was very convenient for carrying extra gear, like the maternity bag.

Memory awakes to one evening of much snow and blizzard, when I was feeling somewhat fatigued, after spending most of the night out at a confinement. On my way to bed at 10 pm, the telephone rang. One of my patients in Cushnie booked to go to a local maternity hospital, was snowed up. Collecting the district nurse for that area, we charged the snow wreaths with the old Dodge and managed to get as far as the Cushie shop. There we met the father-to-be, and dumping one of the bags on him, proceeded to walk in very deep snow across country to the farm where the confinement was to take place. I would have taken to my skis, but as the nurse could not manage this progression, I lent her a ski stick to help her walking. In the morning, we departed for home at 6 am, having delivered a bonnie wee girl. The farmer whose land we crossed, seeing the imprints of the ski sticks remarked, 'Fatna queer-like b____ o' a beast has been here?' This patient gave me a nasty fright, as just as we were departing, she started a post-partum haemorrhage. Happily we got it stopped in a very short time.

THE GREAT GALE OF JANUARY 1953

On 31 January 1953, I woke in the morning to a constant series of cracking sounds and at each one, a fully grown tree snapped at about twelve feet from the ground and left a jagged spike. The gale was cruel and of course the day became known as the great windblow, and laid countless acres of forests in Scotland to devastation. I had promised myself the last day of the shooting season that year, but on seeing the day, I went down to the surgery to see what help could be given to my assistant. Telephone poles were snapped all down the road and the wires were in a tangled confusion. The main road was blocked with fallen trees, but I was granted the courtesy of going through the Littlewood drives. No telephone communication had been possible with my assistant. On arriving at the surgery, he informed me that a local tradesman had sustained a nasty head injury when in collision with a lorry while on the way to Alford. As the injury was about the temple, the doctor sent him by ambulance to Aberdeen Royal Infirmary, but every road was blocked by trees and snow. Eventually the ambulance arrived back on my doorstep at Brux. the patient said, 'I'm awfu caul', could ye tak me in for a heat at the fire?' This we did immediately, but we still had to try to get him into hospital. We tried Huntly next, but with no more success, so I asked the patient whether he would like to come in to Brux or go back to the ambulance base, which was the Forbes Arms Hotel. He said, 'I would like to bide here.' Being very worried about the site of his head injury, I made up my mind to relieve the pressure on his brain, rather than abandon all attempt to save his life. Fortunately, that awful possibility never occurred. I gave my wife strict instructions to examine the size of his pupils every half hour or so. He suddenly said to her 'Eh lassie, ye surely mann hae a notion o' me, aye lookin' in my e'en.' The night passed peacefully, and the violence of the storm blew itself out. Next day was Sunday and we went up to Kildrummy Kirk or as near as we could get with the Land Rover. No other parishioners managed to make it, so we hiked to the manse where we were made welcome by our good minister and his wife, and had a little quiet service with them. Thereafter, the minister and the doctor set out on skis to visit the wife and daughter of the patient who we were harbouring, to reassure them that he was well and would be taken home when the roads and the weather permitted. They were much relieved.

The real tragedy of that awful day, was the sinking of the car ferry *Princess Victoria* on her voyage from Stranraer to Larne. The captain warned that the rear doors would stove in and they should not sail. The owners insisted that the trip must be made, and the resultant loss of life was colossal. All five officers were lost. The captain was last seen at the salute on the deck as the vessel disappeared. the young wireless operator stayed at his post long after he was told to abandon ship and of course, many passengers felt too seasick to try and save themselves. The survivors were mostly old seamen who struggled with the dreadful conditions and were eventually rescued off the coast at Larne, about a mile from their intended destination. I have never ceased to mourn that awful loss, although no individual was known personally to me.

FISHING—THE HEALING BALM

Fishing, I always referred to as the healing balm, for you could stand by the river and be enchanted by the soft sounds of the rippling water, combined with the little noises of the dippers as they skimmed the top of the river alighting on a stone and giving their friendly little call. Other more bossy noises echoed from the hills above, like the grouse and blackcock, while at your feet were the mini creatures like minnows and insects of all sorts. All these things were so soothing after days and nights of hard work and worry. Whether you caught anything or not was not really important, but of course it was pleasant to take home a salmon, apart from the magic moment when you saw it boil at your fly and waited for that enchanting pull that was an invitation into the deep. Then you got going and did your best to keep the fish safely on the end of your line until you could land him. I have almost always tailed my fish by gripping the tail with my hand, exerting firm pressure between my thumb and finger from back to belly. This does not spoil the beauty of the creature in any way. Undoubtedly, fly fishing brings more enchantment than spinning, but when conditions are adverse such as a very big water or it is drummlie and dark, so as to obscure the fly, it may be warranted. Fifty to sixty years ago, we used to fish with a silk line which was greased so that it would float on the water and with quiet skill the fisherman would cast and literally pour it onto the water surface where it flowed out quietly like cream. Nowadays with the floating line artificially constructed, anyone could achieve this. I feel that people could improve their fishing technique by trying the old-fashioned way first. There is such a vast difference in fishing with graceful care and splashing in a rough and ready manner. My father and mother were both very accomplished fishers, and so I may say is my wife, whom I had the pride and pleasure of teaching myself. My instruction to all those whom I have taught, was to get the lift and back cast right and the forward cast will be perfect. Count ONE — and — TWO!

WHEN THE DOCTOR'S APPETITE PAID OFF

One day I received a call to a couple who were helpers in a poultry business to the wife of a cousin of mine, and were much taken up with the length of time birds were kept hanging after slaughter for her household or for the houses of others to whom they were despatched. Of course, these good folk had no idea that the doctor was related to their employers. The wifie suddenly looked up and in a confidentail and revealing manner said, 'But a' fowk that bides in castles, eats a' thin' stinkin'.' I said, 'Oh that's awfu' interestin'.'

During the war, those who lived through the rationing, will remember the great rejoicing when some special titbit was

available. One morning, after surgery, the post arrived
bringing a very delectable Christmas catalogue from Collie's,
the excellent grocers in Aberdeen. Temptation caused me to
dally for a few minutes to look at this, when the phone rang
and fortunately I was still in the surgery, as an urgent call
arrived to say that one of my dear old patients had 'burst her
leg'. This meant that a varicose vein had been opened up
accidentally and of course the blood gushed forth like a river in
spate. Hopping into the old Ford V8, I hastened to her house
at the top of one of the Tullynessle glens. When I arrived
there, a woman was on her knees mopping up the blood as it
flowed over the threshold. Pushing past her, I found my
patient laying back in an old leather chair looking like
alabaster. Seizing a penny from my pocket and wrapping it in
gauze, I pressed it on the vital spot and bandaged firmly.
There was no blood transfusion team to come out in those
days, so the only thing one could do was to send the ambulance
into hospital with the patient forthwith. Having given orders
about all this before leaving home, shortly the vehicle arrived
and the dear wifie was on her way to the Royal Infirmary in
about ten minutes. It was one fortunate time that the lusts of
the flesh did a good turn, as recovery was rapid. A few more
minutes of bleeding might indeed have proved fatal.

WHAT THE DOC KNEW

In the early days in Alford, I felt much more confident about
surgical than medical cases, as this was much more like the
kind of work that occurred in Casualty. Very shortly after
arriving, a call came one dark November evening, for someone
called John, who lived in an old mansion house nearby. I
arrived and rapped on the door about 10 pm. A rather strange
female figure appeared in a flannel nightgown, with long grey
tresses pleated down each side of her head. She had a candle
which she held up and directed a suspicious glance at me, 'Ye'll
be the doctor?' she said and my reply was, 'Aye'. 'Come awa,

it's John, he canna get lyin' doon.' We climbed a bare stone staircase, and all the time I was puzzling why he could not lie down. When we came to the bedroom, which was sparsely furnished, there was an iron bedstead with an old-fashioned black and red blanket and a man propped up on pillows, breathing with discomfort. There was also a collie dog on the bed which growled fiercely and showed its teeth. The housekeeper persuaded the dog to be quiet while I questioned and examined the patient. He was obviously seriously ill with pneumonia so I gave him the only thing which was available to the civil population in those days, sulphathiazole, and told the housekeeper to send for me at any time through the night, but in any case I would return immediately after morning surgery. I felt very depressed when I went away, having the sensation that the dog was very apprehensive that his master was going to die as it growled its farewell message to me. Next morning, on arrival at the big house, I received a kindly smile from the lady, with the words 'a bittie better'. When we reached the bedroom, the collie leaped off the bed and jumped up and licked my face! I was as impressed by this as I had been depressed the previous evening by the dog's behaviour. Things improved every day until finally the housekeeper said with some hesitation, 'Eh Doctor, Spottie has an awfu' sair lug, an we wad be awfu' pleased if ye wad tak a look o' it.' This I did with pleasure as there was no vet available at that time. The dog was full of loving trust and allowed me to do what I wanted. Both patients were soon on the mend.

30TH MEDICAL CLASS REUNION 1939-44

In 1974, our Medical Class reached its 30th year reunion, which took place at Coylumbridge Hotel, Aviemore on 19 October. I was highly honoured to be asked by my old colleagues to speak at the dinner. I have often been asked for a copy of my speech, but such a thing is not in my possession, as I never make up a speech beforehand, feeling it comes in a

Menu

Toast List

The Queen - - - The Chairman

Alma Mater - - Dr. Janet Barry

Reply - - Professor R. D. Lockhart

The Guests - - The Rt. Hon. Sir Ewan Forbes of Brux, Bt.

Reply - - Professor Sir Dugald Baird

not old, but mellow, like good wine"

Coronets of Smoked Salmon Filled with Prawns

Turtle Soup with Sherry and Golden Straws

Fillet of Beef en Croute Truffled Red Wine Sauce Fine Beans Tossed in Butter Almond Croquettes

Rum Baba with Fruit Salad

Coffee

UNIVERSITY OF ABERDEEN

1939-44 MEDICAL CLASS
REUNION

COYLUMBRIDGE HOTEL AVIEMORE

October 19th, 1974

Chairman:
Dr LINDSAY J. SYMON

Menu and Toast List, 1939–44 Medical Class Reunion List.

much more spontaneous way straight from the heart. The only thing I wrote in advance was a poem that afternoon in Braid Scots, to propose the toast to the guests. I attach the Menu which was superb, and the Toast List, also a copy of the Doric poem. I remember very clearly saying 'Fun began with Professor Lockhart', and it did! He kept us on our toes, and interested in what might be regarded as a dry subject, but glistening with the brilliance of his superb teaching. I expressed our admiration for Sir Dugald Baird and the wonderful benefit he bestowed upon many of the women who had few gynaecologists and obstetricians to champion their cause in days gone by. Aberdeen was indeed fortunate in having him and Dr Wyper. Our many splendid clinicians and surgeons and lecturers like Professor Young, made us feel tremendously proud and appreciative of having the opportunity of gaining our knowledge at Aberdeen Medical School. How encouraging it was to have people gifted with a sense of humour like Professor Philip in spite of the strain his dedication must have caused him in his heart-rending subject.

REUNION DINNER 19 OCTOBER 1974

Class 39 tae 44
Was trauchled sairly by the war,
We drilled, fire-watched, did ARP
An' warkit hard for oor Degree

Syne we got on at sic a rate,
For oor tutors were sae really great
        an' also truly humble,
As they listened wi' amazin' grace
Tae mony a queer like mumble.

At length the happy time cam roon'
Fan we could don the M.B. goon,
An' kent that we were brithers a'
Tho' oor experience still was sma'

An' here we are fae a' the airts,
An' some hae come fae foreign pairts,
Tae jine in oor quinquennial spree,
Tae sup some wine or barley bree.

Noo Class 39 tae 44,
I wad speir ye one thing more,
Wi' Scottish pride blaw oot yer' chests,
An' toast oor very welcome guests.

FAITH AND TRUST OF EDUCATION
AND RELIGION

What a depth of deep regret there was in the old scholars and lairds, when in the early part of this century, there developed a habit of good middle-class Scots, to send their sons and daughters to be educated in England. They had made a bit of money and considered there was something grand about such a move, although the benefit and soundness of a good Scottish education was of world-wide renown, also it was accompanied by a strong adherence to the Auld Kirk and the sincerity of her ways. Sending youngsters to English public schools implied attendance at morning prayers and eventually joining the Church of England, which was not in keeping with the hereditary upbringing, and lost contact with people who were the backbone of Scotland. Surely our martyrs did not suffer in vain? Osgood McKenzie, the author of *A Hundred Years in the Highlands* writes with great common sense on the subject, educating boys in Scotland if their future life entailed looking after the land or business in their own country. Of course, further education is never lost, but the basic learning should be in the home country, so that they have a thorough and deep understanding of the ways and problems of their homeland. The importance of studying Scots Law has proved its worth to many a Scot. In the same way, belonging to the Kirk of Scotland forms a link and a feeling of trust and understanding with your ain folk. How often have I heard the remark passed, 'They dinna understand for they belang till a different Kirk and Religion.' I recollect so well the words of one of our great past Moderators of the General Assembly, the Revd Dr Archie Watt, preaching at Kildrummy about the Scots travelling the world, and setting down roots in other countries. They took with them their religion and their education and set them down like a rock.

1920s AT CRAIGIEVAR

Lord and Lady Saltoun of two generations back were staying with my parents at Craigievar Castle in the 1920s and were enjoying a cosy relaxing time after dinner with Lady Saltoun sitting in the ingle-neuk in the Banqueting Hall with the Dandie Dinmont Dog close to her and licking all the while. She was most attracted by the fond attention of the little animal, and could not stop speaking about it. Eventually the company made a move to retire to bed, and when the Dandie's beard was revealed in the light, it was a cascade of sapphire jelly. He had been licking Lady Saltoun's beautiful dress of blue sequins, which evidently tasted nice, until the side he was sitting next was completely dissolved to a gel. My mother felt that any form of apology was inadequate. Lord Saltoun was very good and patient with me when I was a wee loon and played Red Indians and made bracken wigwams with me when he got tired of fishing. I still treasure the book he gave me of King Arthur and his Knights, illustrated by Arthur Rackham. The one with Excalibur being drawn from the stone, still fires my imagination.

CURLERS COURT

No story of Fintray House would ever be complete without including the fun of a curler's initiation. The best one I remember was conducted by our very old and dear friend, George 2nd Marquis of Aberdeen, who dressed himself in a wonderful garb, made I believe by Red Indians, when he was in Canada. Every new member initiated was presented with a breem cowe as broom is the badge of the Forbeses, and it was tied with Forbes Tartan. Those already sworn in, laid with gusto to the newcomers, shouting, 'I canna hear ye, speak up tae my Lord.' They were given a violent handling on the old farm-made rocking horse and multi-coloured embellishment was painted on their faces and especially on bald heads. Whenever they opened their mouths evil tasting liquids were squirted in. After everyone was pitten throu' we settled down to a fine 'Beef and Greens' laid on by my mother, followed by a lively Curlers Court with fines into which Lord Aberdeen's little and gentle lady joined in full spirit. I am proud to relate that my father had the honour by being made president of the Royal Caledonian Curling Club.

PROFESSOR ADLER

Earlier on I mentioned Professor Adler, founder of the School of Adlerian Psychology. He was a great friend of my cousins Ernan and Phyllis Forbes Dennis. Being an Austrian Jew, he left Vienna before the Anschluss and went to America, where he took all his medical exams again to enable him to practise in the USA. When writing medical books, he went back to his own language, German, and then sought a translator. In 1937 he came to Aberdeen on a lecture tour for a week. My family and I attended these very interesting lectures at Aberdeen Medical School, and in between lectures, I drove him about the countryside. One place he was very anxious to visit was the

manse at Corgarff, where the old Minister The Revd John
Linton had translated his most recent textbook and he was
delighted with the result. Sadly, the day his last lecture at the
University was due, he collapsed while walking along Diamond
Street, and died immediately of a massive coronary throm-
bosis. He uttered the word 'Kurt' which was the name of his
younger son, about whom he was concerned. He was given a
fitting funeral service at King's College Chapel, with a full
attendance of all the Court.

GROUSE AND HEATHER

All my life I have endeavoured to take my holidays in August to
walk up grouse with a few old friends and enjoy shooting with
my dear dogs. For many years while they were my neighbours,
I had Colonel Bob Herman, late Hussars, and cousin Willie
Sutherland, who were both splendid shots. We never had more
than three guns on the 12th, because it gave us lots of shooting
and lots of exercise. We always went out on a small bit of very
good moor where there was a splendid burnie running through
and on drouthy days, the birds were always sitting near by. In
1958, the 12th of August was beautiful and very hot. We had
the exquisite pleasure of walking on this beautiful purple
carpet with the enchanting smell of heather honey. The grouse
were there in large numbers, but there was no thought of a
record bag. It was only at the end of the day that we discovered
that our total was sixty-eight brace! I had a very good keeper at
that time — John Reid — who had a very special understanding
of game birds and indeed, the same year, our top bag for wild
pheasants on one day was one hundred and seven. Sadly my
old friend Bob Hermon was claimed by intestinal cancer, and
Willie Sutherland gave up shooting on account of a disability.

In my old age, I have some new sporting friends whose
company I enjoy very much, and I have the help of my late
brother's keeper, now retired, whom I fee'd for him many years
ago and he looked after my brother very well when he became

partially paralysed. I have a keen young great-nephew who is a good shot and turning out a good fisherman.

For most of my life, I have had yellow labradors, but twice I had the fun of Weimaraners, which are wonderful pointers, and also a little Welsh spaniel who knew all the answers.